Selling to China

Ker D. Gibbs
Editor

Selling to China

Stories of Success, Failure, and Constant Change

Editor
Ker D. Gibbs
University of San Francisco
San Francisco, USA

ISBN 978-981-99-1952-9   ISBN 978-981-99-1953-6   (eBook)
https://doi.org/10.1007/978-981-99-1953-6

This Palgrave Macmillan imprint is published by the registered company Springer Nature Singapore Pte Ltd.
The registered company address is: 152 Beach Road, #21-01/04 Gateway East, Singapore 189721, Singapore

Dedicated to the memory of Robert "Bob" Theleen (1945–2021)

FOREWORD

If the U.S.-China relationship is the most consequential relationship of the twenty-first century, then getting America's China policy right is one of the century's defining challenges—one that America's prosperity and security, and that of its friends and allies, depends on. Bringing all available resources to getting that policy right is, therefore, critically important. This book is a step toward bringing a well-informed voice into the discussion: the U.S. business community based in China.

Getting China policy "right" has never been easy for the United States. The track record is decidedly mixed. One reason it is hard is because making the right policy choices requires a nuanced understanding of what is happening in China at the local and national level. Particularly with trade and economic issues, a general understanding is insufficient.

When I was in government, I frequently met with business leaders, including some of the authors in this book. I learned from them that each region in China can be very different, and each industry faces its own unique challenges. These challenges have also changed over time. In the 1990s, when I was consul general in the northern industrial city of Shenyang, American companies were struggling for market access. Later, managing growth and finding enough staff were more important considerations. Today, we have an entirely new set of problems, driven largely by the tension between Beijing and Washington.

During my rotations through Washington, it was apparent to me that we don't have nearly enough information about China to make informed policy decisions that will be effective and constructive. The AmCham delegations that visit Washington are always well received, both by the administration and on the Hill. Policymakers are eager to hear directly from practitioners who are managing businesses and working on the ground in China. These are the people who are directly affected and bear the consequences of American actions like the trade war, export controls, and sharp rhetoric.

While my colleagues in the State Department were always eager to meet with business executives, their reaction to the messages was mixed. Some people in the administration felt that business people were naive, or deliberately ignoring the national security and human rights concerns that we have with China. That sentiment was definitely expressed by members of Congress, who would often exchange views with the State Department after the AmCham delegation had met with them.

It is true that businesspeople tend to see things only through a certain lens, but this only highlights how important it is for policymakers to hear views from different constituencies. China is a complicated place, and it is constantly evolving.

China's rapidly changing regulatory and policy environment poses additional challenges because policies that were effective in the past may not be effective now. Over the last few years, some of the most significant policy failures—including the disastrous trade war—were born and allowed to fester, in part, because decision-makers lacked a detailed understanding of what was happening on the ground.

The contributors to this book have spent decades on the ground deciphering China, studying its politics, optimizing supply chains, analyzing consumer preferences, and competing for market share. They have spent years negotiating with Chinese regulators, suppliers, and customers on uneven playing fields against increasingly nimble Chinese firms. In many cases they have better, more consistent access to senior Chinese officials than the U.S. government does and understand how China works and what works in China—and they want to be part of the solution.

To be part of the solution, the U.S. business community in China must make its voice heard in American policy circles. This isn't easy, particularly when travel between the United States and China is so difficult. Yet, as competition becomes the dominant frame of reference for U.S.-China relations, the people and corporations whose jobs and livelihoods require vigorously competing in China can and should play a greater role in informing U.S. policy. This book is a step in this direction.

It was not always so difficult for business to share their views. In the past, the business community had regular opportunities to engage with US officials and lawmakers visiting China. The American Chambers of Commerce in China and organizations like it were useful platforms for business to share insights and dispel dangerous misconceptions. In recent years, however, few U.S. officials have chosen to come to China. China's quarantine rules and COVID-19 control policies have made visits virtually impossible in recent years, but even before COVID-19 the number of U.S. lawmakers and policymakers traveling to China had already slowed to a trickle.

Members of Congress have been lining up to follow House Speaker Nancy Pelosi's visit to Taiwan, but how many of them are willing to travel to the mainland to hear the other side of the story? Congressional delegations used to come through China frequently, but the last one was in 2014. America is a democracy, so these people need to be ever mindful of how things look to their voters, but ignoring China would be a big mistake. This is another reason why this book is important—even as cries that "engagement is dead" echo in the halls of Congress, the authors of this book are what we have left as eyes and ears in China.

There is another important factor keeping American businesses from participating fully in the policy discussions in Washington: persistent misperceptions about the way U.S. companies operate in China, leading to unfounded concerns about their objectivity.

Deep within America's DNA is a belief that American companies in China have a dual responsibility: to generate returns for shareholders and to conduct their operations in a manner consistent with American values. Americans rightly expect companies flying the American flag to operate legally and ethically and not cut corners on worker rights, product safety, or the environment, even if it reduces shareholder returns. Moreover, Americans would strongly object to U.S. companies prioritizing China business over American jobs and economic security. American companies in China strongly agree. Despite this, in some circles there is a mistaken belief that U.S. companies in China have placed profit over principles or sacrificed their values or even national and economic security for market access. This is simply wrong and not born out by the facts.

Ever since China opened its doors to U.S. business and investment four decades ago, American companies have modeled responsible corporate citizenship. American companies not only led the way in providing safe working conditions, guarding the environment, and protecting workers from discrimination and sexual harassment in their own operations, but they insisted that their network of suppliers do so as well, making an enormous difference for countless Chinese workers. Long before the U.S. Congress passed the Uyghur Forced Labor Prevention Act, American companies already required suppliers to meet high ethical standards regarding the treatment of employees. They did not need a law requiring them to do this. They were already doing it. The American public should be proud of U.S. companies' performance and behavior in China.

More importantly, by doing business in China, American companies promote U.S. economic and national security. This isn't a zero-sum proposition. Not only does American business in China support thousands of jobs in the United States and create export markets for American products and services, cutting-edge U.S. firms often rely on revenue from sales in China to fund the R&D that gives them their technological edge. In many industries, being competitive globally requires companies to be present in all major markets—or they won't be globally competitive for long. If U.S. business doesn't engage in the China market, companies from Europe and Asia, including China, would gladly fill the void and grow at America's expense, weakening the U.S. economy, sacrificing American jobs, and jeopardizing American competitiveness around the globe. The American business people competing in China's market help make America's economy strong. Their voices and experience should play a greater role in shaping an effective U.S.-China policy. This book is an important step to make that happen.

Shanghai, China

Mr. Sean B. Stein
Senior Advisor, Covington &
Burling LLP

Sean B. Stein *served as the United States Consul General in Shanghai from 2017 to 2020. He is currently a senior advisor in Covington's Public Policy Practice Group. Stein joined Covington after a twenty-year diplomatic career with the U.S. government, serving in leadership positions in Washington, China, and other parts of Asia. His insights informed policymaking at the highest levels in Washington. He has also assisted dozens of U.S., Chinese, and international firms to develop strategies, manage risk, and identify opportunities for growth in response to the changing U.S.-China relationship. Mr. Stein is the current Chairman of the American Chamber of Commerce in Shanghai.*

The original version of this book was revised: Incorrect country name has been corrected in copyright page. The correction to this book is available at https://doi.org/10.1007/978-981-99-1953-6_10

ACKNOWLEDGMENTS

A book like this is very much a collaborative effort and would not be possible without the work of many people and organizations. On behalf of myself and the other authors, I want to thank those who contributed and brought this work to fruition.

The American Chamber of Commerce in Shanghai has played and continues to play a vital role in educating people about China's business environment and promoting a positive commercial relationship between the United States and China, a task that has become more difficult in recent years. AmCham convenes high-level meetings between business executives and government officials, both from China and the United States, providing a platform for discussing issues and trends.

The authors of this book have all been members of AmCham at one time or another. Some of us also held leadership roles. For myself, I was given the honor of serving on the Board of Governors and eventually became the full-time executive managing Chamber operations and the staff of 50 or so professionals. We wish to thank the Chamber, the Chamber staff, and all those who make AmCham the great institution that it is.

Ken Jarrett was my predecessor as president of the Chamber, a role he took on after a nearly 30-year career as a diplomat with the U.S. government. His guidance and wise counsel over the years have helped not just me, but the entire American business community. He also spent many hours going through the manuscript and helping us clarify important points. We also thank him for contributing the Epilogue.

With great respect, we recognize the work of the late Bob Theleen, an AmCham legend who was my friend and mentor. He touched the lives and business careers of many in our community. His ideas, observations, and insights about China have contributed greatly to this book.

Sean Stein, who graciously provided the Foreword to this book, deserves thanks in several capacities. As the U.S. Consul General in Shanghai during a particularly difficult time, Sean worked closely and tirelessly with the business community, providing information, guidance, and solving all manner of problems. Having left the government for a private sector role, he was elected to the AmCham Board of Governors and serves as the current chair. We thank him for his service to our nation and to our community, and we wish him well in his new role.

We acknowledge and thank the other AmChams in mainland China, of which there are several. AmCham Shanghai, located in the commercial and financial capital of China, is the largest by far with some 3,000 members. AmCham China, located in Beijing, plays an important role because it is close to the central government and the U.S. Embassy. AmCham South, located in Guangzhou, has a large membership in a very dynamic region of China.

AmCham Shanghai collaborates with many organizations, but two that have had a direct impact on the work described in this book are the U.S.-China Business Council (USCBC), based in Washington D.C., and the National Committee on U.S.-China Relations (NCUSCR), based in New York. We wish to thank Ambassador Craig Allen at USCBC, and Jan Berris and Steve Orlins at the NCUSCR, for their tireless support for the American business community in China, and the important work they do for U.S.-China relations.

The U.S. Chamber of Commerce, also based in Washington D.C., is another important sister organization. Charles Freeman, Jeremie Waterman, and others with the U.S. Chamber have been helpful to American business executives, especially on our visits to the capital.

The University of San Francisco (USF) supported this book, providing research materials and other resources. In particular, we wish to thank university president Father Paul Fitzgerald, as well as Professor Xiaohua Yang, the executive director of the Center for Business Studies and Innovation in Asia-Pacific, which is part of the School of Management.

My USF research assistant, Anchal Khandelwal, edited, fact-checked, and moved our work toward completion, all while continuing her own graduate studies in development economics. We thank her for her work on this project and wish her well on projects of her own. Ms. Khandelwal and others helped make corrections to the manuscript, but any mistakes that remain are mine alone, as the editor.

Doing business overseas, especially in a country as different from the West as China, comes with unique challenges, which is very much the point of this book. One of the major differences is the role of government. Both U.S. and Chinese government officials have played important roles in supporting American business operations in China, and we are grateful to both for their invaluable help and support.

The Chinese government, as is discussed in various sections of this book, has supported American businesses operating in China, especially at the sub-national level. While they did not play a role with the book specifically, we wish to thank the many Chinese government officials, especially at the municipal and provincial levels, who have guided and supported our companies and provided a positive climate in which to invest in China.

There are issues between our countries, mainly between the governments at the national level, but there are many, many Chinese officials and individuals who very much want our countries to find a path back to a more cooperative and amicable relationship. Despite the rhetoric between the United States and China, there remains a layer of Chinese government officials who appreciate the many contributions American companies have made to the development of China. They see the best future for their nation and their people being one that is outward-looking and highly integrated with the global economy. In such a future, American companies and foreign executives would continue to play an important role in China.

American government officials have very much supported the work we do, and our presence in China would not be possible without them. They also support our families. The U.S. Consulate in Shanghai has been our main point of contact, helping American citizens with everything from registering births and marriages to more mundane, and at times unpleasant tasks.

The U.S. ambassadors to China have always been supportive, making a point to visit AmCham and exchange views with our members. In particular, Max Baucus and Terry Branstad spent a great deal of time with us in China, for which we are grateful. Clark "Sandy" Randt also deserves special mention, both for his contribution as the longest-serving ambassador to China (2001–2009), but also for his advice on parts of the manuscript. Beyond the Consulate and the Embassy, there are countless other departments and individuals doing important work in Washington, Beijing, and elsewhere that we as business people rely on and could not function properly without.

Several people read the full manuscript, or parts of it, and provided helpful comments. Huge thanks go to Stuart Rauch, a professional writer who worked on this book pro bono, as well as Andres Batista, William White, and of course our editor at Palgrave Macmillan, Jacob Dreyer. Thanks also to Brook Wessel, Michael Pope, John Van Fleet, Bob Ching, John Coughlan, Bob Marshall, and Fraser Howie, who supported this project from the beginning. Many other individuals contributed to this book in various ways, either supporting our companies or helping us as business people and now authors. They know who they are; we are grateful to them.

CONTENTS

List of Contributors

Mark Fischer CEO of Fischer Sports & Entertainment. Boston MA, USA

Ker D. Gibbs Executive in Residence, University of San Francisco. San Francisco, USA

Kenneth Jarrett Senior Advisor, Albright Stonebridge Group. Washington DC, USA

Daniel M. Krassenstein Global Supply Chain Director at Procon Pacific. Lombard IL, USA

Jean Liu Chief Corporate Affairs Officer at EF Education First China. Shanghai, China

Bill Russo CEO of Automobility. Shanghai, China

Bryce Whitwam Former Greater China CEO at Wunderman. New York, USA

Don S. Williams Partner at Hogan Lovells. Shanghai, China

Marie C. Williams Milstein scholar at Cornell University. Ithaca NY, USA

Chun Hung (Kenneth) Yu Former Vice President, 3M Greater China. Shanghai, China

List of Figures

CHAPTER 1

Introduction: About This Book and Why We Wrote It

Ker D. Gibbs

The United States and China seem headed for conflict. Every day, the headlines describe new reasons to dislike, distrust, and disengage from a country that is also one of the world's largest markets. The relationship between the United States and China has often been called the most consequential bilateral relationship on earth, but it also may be the most fraught with conflict and misunderstanding. For the past several years the relationship has grown steadily worse, with no apparent solution to highly contentious issues involving national security, human rights, and sovereignty.

Commerce has traditionally been the bright spot in the relationship, but the two governments are pulling the countries apart, leaving companies stuck in the middle. The governments of both countries are attempting to bring multinational companies to heel, aligning with their respective goals at the policy level. In the words of U.S. Secretary of State

K. D. Gibbs (✉)
Executive in Residence, University of San Francisco. Shanghai, China
e-mail: ker@gibbs.net

© The Author(s), under exclusive license to Springer Nature
Singapore Pte Ltd. 2023
K. D. Gibbs (ed.), *Selling to China*,
https://doi.org/10.1007/978-981-99-1953-6_1

Antony Blinken, "we believe – and we expect the business community to understand – that the price of admission to China's market must not be the sacrifice of our core values or long-term competitive and technological advantages. We're counting on businesses to pursue growth responsibly, assess risk soberly, and work with us not only to protect but to strengthen our national security."[1]

American businesspeople working in China would strongly object to any suggestion that they are sacrificing American values or acting irresponsibly, just because they are working in China. On the contrary, most see themselves as responsible representatives, eager to share our nation's best practices, whether in terms of worker safety, management principles, or business ethics. American multinational companies are not in the business of selling national security secrets or undermining America's lead in technology. There will always be a few bad actors, but the overwhelming majority of American business people are proud of the fact that they do things the right way—they don't cut corners, they abide by the rules, and they respect the rights of individuals.

However, as much as we all might like to see the world made safe for American-style democracy, most business people don't see that as their mission. America's national security is important to all of us, but this must be primarily the responsibility of government, not business. Business people certainly work *with* government officials, both American and Chinese, and fully cooperate with relevant rules and policies. But business and government are two different things.

Just as Secretary Blinken sees a certain role for American business in the relationship, Chinese officials have become more forceful with their guidance as well. China's ambassador to the United States, Qin Gang, met with business leaders in Shanghai in July of 2021 on his way to taking up his duties in Washington DC. He told us we should play a more active role in explaining to our government that its efforts to decouple from China are misguided and unhelpful. While our group certainly shared his concern about the negative effects of decoupling, we were obliged to point out that Beijing plays a role in this as well. What is China's so-called Great Firewall, if not an effort to silo the internet and keep China and its digital economy separate from the rest of the world?

---

[1] https://www.state.gov/the-administrations-approach-to-the-peoples-republic-of-china/

In China, cooperation with government—and compliance—has become more challenging. Global companies are having increasing difficulty managing export controls, sanctions, and counter-sanctions. The cost of meeting regulatory directives has increased dramatically in recent years, and these costs are felt disproportionately by small and medium-sized enterprises. America's Uyghur Forced Labor Protection Act is one example of a U.S. law that will be extremely difficult for importers to comply with, but there are also Chinese laws, such as the cybersecurity law that mandates the localization of data that are vague and change frequently, putting foreign companies in a bind.

THE AMERICAN CHAMBER OF COMMERCE

The American Chamber of Commerce in Shanghai, or AmCham, plays an active role in helping companies sort through these and other challenges. AmCham is a place where CEOs, entrepreneurs, lawyers, and bankers come together to exchange information and express views. It is also the focal point for government officials to meet with business leaders. AmCham has held countless meetings with Chinese officials at all levels, and much of what we have learned at these meetings is reflected in this book.

AmCham has made a point of maintaining close relationships with the U.S. ambassador to China and has hosted visiting members of Congress and cabinet-level officials from the executive branch of our government. The Chamber organizes an annual trip to Washington DC, known as the "Doorknock," where we meet members of Congress and administration officials who have expressed great interest in hearing from business people who live and work in China. We meet with the Department of Commerce, Treasury, and Agriculture, as well as the U.S. Trade Representative's office. Several of the authors in this book have participated in this delegation and have shared what they learned from the meetings.

THE AUTHORS

The American business community in China is deeply concerned about the downward spiral that seems to be pulling the two nations closer to open conflict. Such a conflict would wipe out decades of investment and hard work and deny future opportunities for job growth and value creation. But at this point, that is actually not our biggest concern.

Ripping apart our two economies would be bad for business, but a direct military conflict between the United States and China would be catastrophic.

We, meaning the individual authors of this book as well as myself as the editor, are worried about this threat, and we believe there is a layer of information missing from the discussion. In any democracy, the general public—the voting public—needs to have a full set of facts and a complete picture, especially on issues as complicated and consequential as those that involve the United States and China. Company boards and advisors may find other useful information in these pages that will guide them as their businesses face certain operating challenges. Policymakers too may look at China from a different angle, but our goal remains the same: we want to do everything in our power to provide information about the commercial side of the U.S.-China relationship, which we see as an important and stabilizing influence.

As the editor, I invited these authors because each one has a unique story to tell and can explain in their own words how foreign companies are operating in China and the challenges they face. Each of them has led a business of substantial size or importance and done so from on the ground in China—not from headquarters. These people know of what they speak.

The authors all managed foreign businesses, but they are not necessarily foreigners. Some were born in China, others not. This reflects the reality that American companies in China are largely run by local people, not foreigners. In the early days, American multinationals sent dozens of expats to China to manage local operations. Over the years, as the skill level of Chinese workers came up, and the tolerance for paying the high cost of expats went down, management teams have become more local. Adding to this, the travel restrictions associated with COVID-19 have caused extreme difficulty for foreign employees and their families, resulting in an acceleration in the departure of Americans working in China.

Could the fact that American companies are no longer managed by Americans be what Secretary Blinken was referring to? I've seen no evidence to support the claim that Americans who work in China abandon their values, but American *companies* would have only limited influence on the values of the local people who work there. Companies can certainly screen for and train behaviors, but changing values and beliefs is a different matter.

I was also careful to invite only those who I knew would speak their mind, as opposed to pushing out sanitized corporate talking points. Sadly, it was not easy to convince everyone to agree to be included in this book. The authorities in China are extremely sensitive. The leadership in Beijing—and to a large extent the Chinese people as well—believe they are under attack, and that China is misunderstood. Ironically, this has caused the authorities to block nearly everything written about China and punch back against any views that don't conform to the narrative put forward by the Chinese Communist Party, even those that are intended to be constructive and helpful. As a result, businesspeople are hesitant to say anything at all about China, thus adding to the problem of China being misunderstood.

Another way in which China is misunderstood arises because we tend not to be specific when describing the country from afar. It is enormous of course and extremely diverse, and it is formed by many component parts, even within the narrow context of business. When we say "China" we're typically referring to the body politic, but the views and aspirations of ordinary Chinese people can be very different from the opinions of their leaders, just as it is elsewhere. We may also use the term "Beijing" when we mean the government, but even the government is distinct from the party. The Chinese Communist Party, or CCP, is not the same as the bureaucracy itself, and in a one-party system it plays a very different role from political parties in the United States. The Democratic Party, for example, currently occupies the White House and has a great deal of influence, but it does not appoint the head of oil companies, commercial banks, or TV stations. In China, the CCP does all that and more.

THE ROLE OF GOVERNMENT

This brings us to the first, and perhaps the most important, theme in this book: the role of government. Most of the chapters address this in various ways, but our corporate affairs expert Jean Liu has written a short yet remarkably comprehensive guide to how multinationals interact with Chinese officialdom. Foreign companies in China employ large, highly paid government relations teams. These people are often recruited from government departments. In the United States, this function tends to be part of corporate communications or public affairs, but in China the government relations team typically reports directly to the CEO and is often responsible for generating business. The China CEO role itself is largely about maintaining relationships with Chinese officials.

The role of government in China is also one of its most controversial and contentious issues with the United States and other Western democracies within the realm of trade. Beijing manages the economy using very different tools than those employed in the United States. China's state-owned enterprises and industrial subsidies are key levers of control that its leaders are unlikely to give up – even if they violate the rules of the WTO, or might end up keeping China out of major multilateral trade agreements like the Comprehensive and Progressive Agreement for Trans-Pacific Partnership (CPTPP).

That is a problem for Beijing to work out with the governments of other nations, but in company boardrooms the question is how to operate legally within this system to maximize shareholder value.

In China Selling to China

Another theme that is particularly relevant to company boards is the evolution of how American companies are organized. The structure of American businesses in China changed as China's needs and capabilities evolved. After the normalization of U.S.-China relations in 1979, business began with simple imports. There was some assembly being done locally, but staff in China were mainly focused on sales and distribution. Very little was produced in China, and there was certainly no product development.

In the 1980s and early 1990s, most foreign companies were forced into joint ventures with local firms. Usually, the partners were state-owned enterprises with very different working cultures and business objectives, as Daniel Krassenstein points out in his chapter on supply chains.

Over time, especially after China entered the World Trade Organization in 2001, foreign companies invested aggressively in China. This set China on the path to becoming the world's factory, with everything from umbrellas to televisions being made in China. Now, as Krassenstein explains, other countries are emerging to challenge China's position, with mixed success.

In the late 1990s and 2000s, as Chinese society became more wealthy, foreign firms shifted toward viewing China as a key market. They began serving China's consumer needs as well as those of industry. This gave rise to the slightly ambiguous term "in China *for* China," replacing the term "made *in* China." The new wording was meant to emphasize the idea that foreign companies had a long-term commitment to China, and that they were there for the domestic market as opposed to exploiting cheap labor for manufactured exports. Over time, and as U.S.-China relations deteriorated, the new term became awkward. People in Washington began to construe the term—perhaps deliberately—in a way that seemed to call into question the loyalty of American firms. Election cycles in America now regularly feature politicians bringing up issues with China as a way to rouse voters. Several of our authors here point out how this rhetoric actually damages American interests in the long term.

As China developed, the capabilities of local firms increased dramatically. Foreign firms found that in some instances they could no longer compete successfully against their local counterparts. The domestic market has become more sophisticated and consumer tastes more local, giving additional weight to the home court advantage that exists in China as it does almost everywhere. In some cases, foreign companies report the existence of an unlevel playing field and barriers to entry, adding to the difficulties faced by foreign competitors. Some have settled for minority equity stakes in their would-be competitors, while others have taken on local partners or opted for licensing deals. This gave rise to yet another slogan, "in China *with* China." Still, the majority of foreign companies would describe themselves today as "in China selling to China."

The title of this book was chosen to highlight this point. Most American businesses view China primarily as a market, and an opportunity to sell goods and services. Again, as our chapter on supply chains explains, China is no longer a source of cheap labor. China's labor force has in fact been shrinking since it peaked in 2014. The buying power of its growing middle class has increased exponentially in recent years, so today the country is attractive to foreign companies above all because it is a market for our products and services.

INDUSTRY TRENDS

There may be no industry that provides a better example of "selling to China" than automotive, or as our industry expert Bill Russo calls it, the "business of mobility." China is the world's largest market for vehicles of all sorts, but the even more significant part of the story is about the innovation that is taking place. China is now the global market leader in new energy vehicles and is developing self-driving cars, battery-as-a-service, and other innovations.

Companies like Tesla have taken advantage of the fact that China has dropped the equity caps in most industries, allowing foreign firms to have complete control over their operations. Tesla operates as a wholly-owned subsidiary in China, which better fits its company culture. Other car manufacturers are still in joint ventures with state-owned enterprises. Some foreign companies entering the market today see value in partnering with local firms, although today they have far more choices than early entrants had.

Going Asset Light

Now, with China threatening to invade Taiwan, American businesses need to reevaluate the structure of their businesses once again. We have just witnessed Russia's shocking invasion of its neighbor, Ukraine. Like Taiwan is today, Ukraine was peaceful, democratic, and threatened no one, but suddenly tanks came across its borders and families were forced from their homes.

American corporations doing business in Russia found themselves in an awkward position, most choosing to withdraw immediately from a nation that has become a global pariah, not wanting to further enable a war machine or give comfort to a regime that will eventually be brought to justice for crimes against humanity. What lessons will American businesses operating in China draw from this? McDonald's, Pepsi, ExxonMobil, and many others—all of which have substantial operations in China as well—closed doors in Russia and had to write billions of dollars off their balance sheets.

It remains to be seen how this could affect American companies investing in China, where companies like GM and Ford have massive balance sheet exposure. While it is unlikely that they will give up the market in the immediate term, over time those that can may shift to a more asset-light model, putting less of their own capital at risk.

TECHNOLOGY, INNOVATION, AND THEFT OF INTELLECTUAL PROPERTY

In the early days of China's opening up, the leadership was desperate to build up the economy as quickly as possible in any way they could. In the 1980s and 1990s, intellectual property rights were generally ignored. This development path was not entirely different from that of other countries, including the United States. Americans in the 1800s were famous for stealing intellectual property to build cotton mills, so much so that guards were stationed at British ports to prevent people with specialized knowledge from leaving the country.

Today, China's system for protecting intellectual property is well developed, as lawyer Don Williams explains in his chapter on legal services. He argues that pressure from foreign nations may have played a part but this shift also coincides with China becoming an owner of IP that it wants to protect. Either way, a problem like this is never completely solved, and foreign companies continue to rank the issue of IP protection high on their list of priorities.

Technology is a major theme that appears in all the chapters of this book. Bryce Whitwam, our marketing guru, describes the remarkable shifts in the social media landscape in China, and how his advertising clients have responded to take advantage of these trends. Global companies see China as a source of innovation and consumer trends. They know that their next competitor is likely to be from China, so they are understandably eager to be in the market in order to stay current and competitive. We all need to understand what is happening, as strange phenomena like China's TikTok app arrive on our shores.

China has made a deliberate move to leapfrog analog solutions and go entirely digital throughout the country. To a degree that shocks (and inconveniences) visitors, Chinese consumers eschew paper and coins and use mobile phone payments almost exclusively. In this and other ways, China's use of technology is in fact far ahead of most nations. China's leaders understand that with a shrinking population, productivity gains are the only way to maintain growth, so they have pushed for a 100% digital economy. Citizens have no choice but to comply, but very few actually object, even though they give up privacy and hand the government a great deal of control. The private sector has embraced and fueled China's leap into the age of digital technology, creating huge wealth in the process.

Separating from China—the so-called decoupling that concerns us— would leave global companies oblivious of trends that are sweeping China in every sector and could arrive in our home markets soon. Author Kenneth Yu offers his perspective on local competition and explains how 3 M found business opportunities in the market in unexpected ways. The capabilities of local firms have increased dramatically, and foreign companies are losing the contest for the best talent. These challenges are exacerbated by geopolitical tensions.

People, Culture, and Competition

No business book on China would be complete without some discussion of culture and the unique characteristics of the Chinese people. Mark Fischer, the executive who brought the NBA to China, shares some astute observations about the strengths and weaknesses in the culture relevant to competitive sports. As a semi-pro basketball player himself, he explains lessons from his unique experience both on and off the court.

Fischer describes the amazing journey of the NBA in China, including how Chinese consumers and brands embraced one of America's favorite pastimes, only to shun NBA games after an off-hand tweet about China's internal politics. As strong as China appears to be as a nation, it is remark- ably fragile and hypersensitive to outside criticism on anything it considers a domestic affair.

Several authors address the question of Chinese "face," and how things can go horribly wrong when Chinese people are criticized publicly. Showing respect is essential in any business relationship. Several authors also offer their own interpretation of the Chinese concept of "guānxi" (关系) and how relationships come into play.

Making the Case for Trade

The authors of this book address many different topics, but all of them— all of us—are making the case for trade. Consumers in the United States buy inexpensive products made in China, enabling them to enjoy a better lifestyle while leaving more cash in their wallets. Practically everything sold at Walmart and Home Depot is made in China. Trade has been good for both countries.

We recognize that these benefits from trade have not been shared evenly across the United States. People with lower incomes spend less on consumer items, with the bulk of their income going for food, housing, and other necessities that are not traded goods. Wage-earners in manufacturing jobs have been hurt by trade with China. Economists claim that displaced workers should naturally shift to better paying, higher value-added industries, but that simply hasn't happened. People don't go from metal-bending jobs to working at Facebook. Wages in the United States have stagnated for the past thirty years, which almost exactly coincides with our trade with China.

Voters in the United States have become anti-trade; trade has become synonymous with China, so people have become anti-China. There may be many non-commercial reasons to take issue with China, and Beijing and its wolf-warrior diplomats[2] are not helping their own case. But would *not* trading with China result in higher wages for American workers? Keeping China out of WTO may have slowed the trend, but it would be hard to make the argument that cutting off trade with China today would be good for the American worker.

OUR HOPE FOR THE FUTURE

Our goal with this book is to provide readers with a more nuanced understanding of China and the environment in which foreign businesses operate there. The intent is not to lay blame on one side or another for the uncomfortable situation we are in. On the contrary, our hope is for Chinese and non-Chinese readers to develop more understanding and appreciation for how the issues might be viewed by "the other side."

For the past four decades, the United States and China have lived in relative peace. This peace has enabled and nurtured a commercial relationship that has made both countries more prosperous than they would have been on their own. It is undoubtedly desirable—and still possible— for the two countries to find a path forward that each can comfortably live with.

Resolving our issues would lead to the best possible outcome and usher in a new age of prosperity for both nations. The last four decades have demonstrated that cooperation between the United States and China is possible and highly productive. Working together would lead to advances

---

[2] Wolf warrior diplomacy, or *zhànláng wàijiāo* (战狼外交), describes China's aggressive style of diplomacy adopted under Xi Jinping. The term comes from the Chinese action film, *Wolf Warrior.*

in how we manage everything from climate change, global pandemics, resources in the arctic, and many other areas of mutual interest.

Choices are being made now that will shape the relationship between the United States and China for years to come, and the outcome will be felt everywhere on earth. We hope those choices will take us in the direction of more trade, more jobs, more prosperity, and above all peace for both nations.

Ker D. Gibbs *is the immediate past president of the American Chamber of Commerce in Shanghai, where he focused on U.S.-China relations and business issues facing American companies operating in Asia. Mr. Gibbs has lived in Asia for more than two decades and is a Mandarin speaker. In the 1990s, Mr. Gibbs worked for the Boston Consulting Group in Shanghai and San Francisco. Since then, he has split his time between Asia and Silicon Valley, serving in executive positions with Apple, Disney, and high-growth Internet businesses. He moved to Shanghai in 2002 as head of Asia Pacific for a Nasdaq-listed network security company that was acquired by McAfee. His career in high tech led him to banking, where he became head of technology and media in Greater China for HSBC. As an investment banker, he advised at the board and C-level at Alibaba, Baidu, and other firms engaged in mergers and cross-border transactions. From banking, Mr. Gibbs moved to direct investments. He was a founding investor in the Crystal Orange Hotel Group, helping grow the company to 130 properties and 1,500 employees in China. He also led successful investments in real estate, e-commerce, and medical technology companies. Before his appointment as president, Mr. Gibbs served on the Board of Governors of the American Chamber of Commerce in Shanghai for four years, including two years as chairman. He sat on the audit committee, finance committee, and compensation committee. Other board roles include tech/social media companies MyETone and the Asia joint venture of NBC. He served previously on the board of the United Way in China, a joint venture with the Shanghai Charity Foundation. Currently, he is an Executive in Residence at the University of San Francisco and is a member of the National Committee on U.S.-China Relations. He also sits on the Advisory Board of the Shanghai Jiao Tong University business school and is an Economic and Technology Consultant to the Wuxi Municipal Government in China. He is an op-ed contributor to the Wall Street Journal, South China Morning Post, and other publications. Ker Gibbs holds a BA in economics from UCLA and an MBA from the Haas School of Business at UC Berkeley. He lives in San Francisco and Shanghai.*

CHAPTER 2

Legal Services: Lessons of a Technology Lawyer in China

Don S. Williams and Marie C. Williams

In February 2006, I left the San Francisco Bay Area to move to Shanghai and open the first China office of Wilson Sonsini, a leading Silicon Valley law firm. My decision to move was informed by a calculated gamble on two key macro-level trends—the continued development of China's legal services industry and the further growth and development of China's technology industry. The vision was to offer Silicon Valley-style legal services to China's burgeoning technology sector.

Over the course of almost two decades running a law business dedicated to serving the technology industry in China, my role as a participant in these two sectors has proved to be highly educational. I have seen and learned a tremendous amount about China, its legal services industry, the technology business in China as a whole, intellectual property in

D. S. Williams (✉)
Partner at Hogan Lovells. Shanghai, China
e-mail: don.williams@hoganlovells.com

M. C. Williams
Milstein scholar at Cornell University. Ithaca NY, USA

© The Author(s), under exclusive license to Springer Nature Singapore Pte Ltd. 2023
K. D. Gibbs (ed.), *Selling to China*,
https://doi.org/10.1007/978-981-99-1953-6_2

13

China, and the interaction between the American and Chinese technology sectors. My time "in the trenches" has given me what I believe to be a relatively unique knowledge base and perspective, at least among Westerners, that I hope to share here—in this chapter, I will attempt to distill my observations from my time in China during this remarkable period and also share my analysis of how, moving forward, rising U.S.-China tensions can be expected to continue to impact those areas.

The Legal Industry in China

By 2015, China's legal services sector was already the third largest in the world, though it essentially did not even exist when I graduated from Stanford in 1989.[1] The absence of lawyers at the time stemmed from the Party's then "suspicious if not outright hostile attitude towards the country's lawyers," who since the People's Republic of China's founding in 1949, the Party had believed posed "a potential threat" to their absolute rule.[2] During the Cultural Revolution, lawyers were directly persecuted and condemned, and it wasn't until Deng came into power years later that the country began passing regulations to revitalize the once extinct industry. Given this historical backdrop, all of the remarkable development of the Chinese legal industry has occurred during my adult lifetime, and most of it in front of my very eyes as a practitioner on the ground there since 2005.

China's first private law firm, Jin Mao, was established on December 24th, 1988, ten years after Deng's Reform and Opening.[3] Several leading Chinese law firms today, including Jun He, Fangda, and King & Wood Mallesons, were established during the early 1990s. Yet, while these firms have grown to become powerhouses, in their early days they were quite small and did not have sophisticated capabilities comparable to many of the foreign firms that had expanded into China's legal services market.

The legal services market wasn't at all open to foreign firms until relatively recently, however. The Chinese government did not officially allow foreign law firms to establish offices in China until July 1st of

---

[1] Statista, "Global revenue of the legal services industry by country and region 2015," July 2022.

[2] https://thepractice.law.harvard.edu/article/foreign-firms-china/.

[3] First Law International Official Website.

1992,[4] when it became clear, as stated by a member of China's Ministry of Justice, that an opening of the market would be necessary to "meet the demands of economic development and legal exchange."[5] Numerous restrictions were put in place to limit the activity of these incoming firms, but many still chose to expand to China, and by April of 2001, 103 foreign law firms had been authorized to open representative offices in China.[6]

Despite the significant restrictions placed on them, many foreign firms were rather successful, particularly in the 1990s and early 2000s. American and British firms like Baker & McKenzie, Coudert Brothers, Clifford Chance, and White & Case were successful early on, thanks to their being established in Hong Kong prior to China's official opening. O'Melveny & Myers and Jones Day were also two notable law firms during that time period. Today, many of the relatively successful foreign firms are still from the United States and the UK.[7]

Unfortunately, severe restrictions continue to limit foreign law firms' practice in China. To this day, foreign firms are not allowed to practice Chinese law—most foreign law firms instead advise clients on the Chinese legal environment, aid in transactions such as mergers and acquisitions governed by foreign law that involve Chinese companies, and advise on matters concerning foreign legal compliance. It follows that Chinese lawyers hired by international firms face license suspensions as they too lose the right to practice Chinese law. Additionally, foreign firms are not allowed to engage with certain Chinese government agencies, suffer higher tax rates for their partners (as compared to PRC firms), and face time-consuming registration processes that hinder their ability to hire and grow.[8] There have been some recent favorable changes within the

---

[4] It's worth noting that foreign legal services did exist in China starting in the 1980's, though they labeled themselves as "business representatives" or "consulting firms." Baker McKenzie was one such firm.

[5] Jane Heller, "China's New New Foreign Law Firm Regulations: A Step in the Wrong Direction," *Washington International Law Journal*, Vol. 12, No. 03, May 2003.

[6] Ibid.

[7] Zhong Lun Law Firm, "Ranking the Top Domestic and Foreign Firms in China—A Snapshot of the Present as a Basis for a Projection of Future Market Trends," *The Lawyer*, July 2013.

[8] https://thepractice.law.harvard.edu/article/foreign-firms-china/. This article existed in an earlier issue of Harvard University's *The Practice* magazine, which they will be

Shanghai Free Trade Zone (i.e., joint ventures that are partially or even majority owned by foreign firms can practice PRC law) but these are in the early stages. By contrast, PRC firms in the United States can operate without restriction (assuming their employees are licensed to practice the applicable state's law), hiring whomever they choose and practicing American law.

With their local connections and legal obstacles in place preventing foreign firms from truly flourishing in China, Chinese firms have grown immensely in recent years, even gaining recognition at the international level. Where no Chinese law firm had more than 100 licensed lawyers in 2002, by 2022 around ten had thousands employed.[9] This remarkable transformation of local firms—from laggards to an internationally competitive force in just 15 years—has of course been mirrored across China's economy, in sector after sector. Top Chinese firms are generating billions of dollars of revenue every year,[10] and some have even acquired large Western firms—Dacheng acquired Dentons in November of 2015, and King & Wood acquired Mallesons Stephen Jaques in 2012.[11] Both acquisitions have been widely viewed as successful, and Dentons (Dacheng) was as of 2022 one of the top global firms by revenue.

In short, after just three decades of remarkable development, China's legal sector is now among the world's largest. But that growth has not been evenly shared. Aided by legal restrictions on their foreign rivals, Chinese firms have come to dominate the industry. Foreign firms retain a significant presence in the market, but their early leadership has been supplanted by local players. For many foreign firms at least—and by contrast to a decade ago—China is no longer perceived as the key market for future growth. Moreover, a significant portion of the top foreign legal talent that has helped enable the extraordinarily rapid development of China's legal sector is leaving the country. Shanghai in particular previously attracted smart, ambitious practitioners from overseas with its sophisticated urban landscape, history, culture, and career opportunities.

---

adding back to the website soon. The provided link may be redirected to the magazine's home page until they make the issues available online again.

[9] https://thepractice.law.harvard.edu/article/rise-big-law-china/. See above note.

[10] https://thepractice.law.harvard.edu/article/in-the-news-september-2016/. See footnote 8.

[11] https://thepractice.law.harvard.edu/article/rise-big-law-china/. See footnote 8.

Many of my friends in the foreign bar have now left, and gatherings of overseas lawyers are just a shadow of a decade ago. I understand the city of Shanghai is concerned about the exodus of foreign legal talent and is considering measures intended to reverse the trend. On the other hand, the national government has a stated policy of developing local legal talent and relying less on foreigners.[12] Where this will ultimately lead is hard to say, but for now at least, the era of China as a magnet for foreign legal talent appears to be over.

Notwithstanding the above, there remain opportunities for foreign lawyers and firms in the PRC. Foreign investment into China remains considerable, and some of those investors are more comfortable dealing with foreign law firms they perceive as still having a more rigorous and higher quality service offering, particularly for highly complex transactions. Moreover, by leveraging the aforementioned favorable changes in the Shanghai Free Trade Zone, foreign firms can tap practice areas that have historically been closed to them. Since PRC firms can operate without restriction in the United States and many other Western markets, the PRC government should be encouraged—in the name of further opening up as has been seen recently in the finance and internet financial information services sectors—to grant reciprocity and accelerate recent favorable developments such as in the Shanghai Free Trade Zone.[13]

Should the trend of worsening relations between the United States and China continue, however, it may be unlikely for us to see such favorable changes in the legal services industry, where the market has historically been closed to foreign firms. This has certainly been a concern of American firms, for whom China may no longer be perceived as a key market for future growth. On the other hand, if U.S.-China relations improve, the size and continued development of China's legal industry may still provide opportunities for foreign firms with the patience, resources, and commitment to play for the long term.

---

[12] "Xi stresses rule of law, cultivating legal talent," Xinhua News, May 2017.

[13] "China's 2022 Negative List for Market Access: Restrictions Cut, Financial Sector Opening," *China Briefing*, April 2022.

The Growth of China's Technology Sector

The contrast between forms of everyday payment accepted in China today and twenty years ago serves as a constant reminder of the immense technological advancements the country has made, both in the mobile payment industry and elsewhere. When I first began to spend long periods in Shanghai in 2005, my wallet—bursting with coins and wads of cash out of necessity—was with me everywhere I went, eating a hole in more than a few pants pockets. Few if any establishments accepted credit cards, so cash was the only option. The painstaking counting of change was required for every purchase. Fast forward less than two decades, and my stuffed, bulky wallet is a thing of the past—I now generally only carry my phone when I leave home in Shanghai, and my purchases happen instantaneously without any counting of currency. Alipay, Wechat Pay, and other forms of mobile payment have become ubiquitous to the point where street vendors and even the occasional person on the street asking for money will put up a QR code linking to their e-payment account. This remarkable advancement has been mirrored across many sectors of China's economy during this time period.

Over the last two decades, China's economy has grown at an unprecedented rate. Much of this growth is owed to China's flourishing technology sector, which as of 2020, accounted for about 30% of the country's GDP.[14] Leading companies, though young, have become giants that are now recognized as global leaders in their fields, in some instances surpassing even Western companies that have traditionally led the way. But this was not always the case.

Not long ago, China's tech sector consisted of "copycat" companies that largely imitated the innovations that came out of Western markets. The government protected companies like Baidu as they slowly gained insights from foreign companies and found their footing in the Chinese market. Though much has changed since, and the Chinese tech sector is far more innovative than imitative today, portions of it are still quite dependent on foreign technology.

The Chinese government's role in advancing the country's tech sector has been and continues to be significant. Through a variety of top-down government directives, protectionism, generous industrial subsidies,

---

[14] "What's Pushing China's Tech Sector So Far Ahead?" *Knowledge at Wharton*, October 2019.

and, according to some, state-sanctioned and facilitated industrial espionage, the Chinese government has created an environment where its companies can thrive. For example, the relatively recently enacted Made in China 2025 plan, a state-led industrial policy, is meant to propel even more growth—it aims to make China "self-sufficient in high technology output" and help place China in the leading position in various technology sectors.[15]

But government involvement is only part of the story. A number of other factors have also contributed to the Chinese tech sector's rapid growth. Venture capital funds, many from Silicon Valley, have helped enable the growth and success of a great many Chinese tech companies. Alibaba and Baidu are early examples. Newer big-name companies funded in part by Silicon Valley investors include TouTiao, MeiTuan, DiDi, and XiaoMi among many others. Silicon Valley's expertise in building startups also undoubtedly helped China's technology sector to thrive, particularly in the early days. Other growth-driving factors include the "entrepreneurial drive of companies" and China's "large base of internet users."[16] Chinese companies have also been particularly innovative with the development of new business models, often adopting untraditional ones or creating their own.

Today, China is a global leader in various high-tech fields like 5G, e-commerce, AI, drones, and telecommunications. In some areas, such as mobile payments, facial recognition AI, and the Internet of Things, it is likely *the* world leader. Its tech sector has come a long way, and even as risks of decoupling and tensions with other countries continue to rise, it looks to be on the uptrend.

Various foreign companies, particularly in tech, recognize the vitality of the Chinese market—they believe that their presence in the Chinese market is critical, especially as the market becomes larger and grows ever more innovative. The importance of China's market is certainly not new to many of these companies. Indeed, even as early as 2009, CEOs of major tech companies like Mark Hurd of HP were already declaring China as their most vital market.[17] Back then, many companies saw

---

[15] Hermione Dace, "China's Tech Landscape: A Primer," Tony Blair Institute for Global Change, January 2020.

[16] Ibid.

[17] "Xi stresses," Xinhua.

China primarily as an avenue through which they could "build the scale, expertise, and business capabilities" they would need to expand to other emerging markets in the early 2000s.[18]

As Chinese tech companies innovate in unique and creative ways— through new business models and more—the Chinese market, and more specifically the intensely competitive aspect of it, has also become "a breeding ground" for companies of "superb capabilities."[19] A technology company that does not compete in China risks being blindsided in other international markets and even at home by Chinese companies emerging from that intense cauldron. Tim Cook, CEO of Apple, whose China business is a fundamental part of the company, has also noted the crucial significance of the Chinese market. He claims, "Our view is that China will be Apple's top market in the world — and not just for sales. It's also the developer community, which is growing faster than any other country in the world. The ecosystem there is very, very strong."[20] In a recent Bloomberg interview, Elon Musk of Tesla was asked where he saw the most vibrant competition in electric vehicles, and he replied that he was "very impressed with the car companies in China and just in general, with companies in China. They're extremely competitive, hardworking and smart." He added that consumers can probably expect to see even more China-made products flowing from the world's manufacturing powerhouse than there are now.[21]

Unfortunately, not all technology companies are able to be a part of this important ecosystem. Numerous foreign companies are blocked by the Chinese government from participating in the crucial China market. This parallels later steps the U.S. government has taken since 2018 to limit Chinese companies' participation in the American market.[22] The

[18] Orit Gadiesh, Philip Leung, and Till Vestring, "The Battle for China's Good-Enough Market," *Harvard Business Review*, September 2007.

[19] George Yeip, "5 Strategy Lessons Companies Can Learn From China," *Forbes*, June 2016.

[20] Taylor Soper, "Apple CEO Tim Cook: China will be our top worldwide market, and not just for sales," Geekwire, October 2015.

[21] Angus Whitley, "Elon Musk Sounds Off on Recession Risk, Twitter Deal and Trump," *Bloomberg*, June 2022.

[22] Kate Fazzini, "Trump is now blacklisting several big Chinese companies—here's what they do and why they are important," CNBC, October 2019.

inability of each country's companies to compete freely in the other presaged the U.S.-China tech war.

The U.S.-China Tech War: Then and Now

Correspondingly, while many consider the U.S.-China tech war a recent phenomenon, in our view it really started as early as 2008, when the first skirmishes between the Chinese government and American tech companies began. Following heightened tensions over China's activities in Tibet, various foreign internet platforms, such as Facebook, Twitter, and Youtube/Google, found themselves blocked in China, ostensibly for censorship reasons, despite having been (in their view) fully in compliance with the Chinese government's censorship expectations.[23] Meanwhile, the Chinese counterparts to these platforms remained accessible in China and elsewhere. Even if this distinction between the treatment of the different platforms rested solely upon the fact that the Chinese government has more control over the content on Chinese platforms and no ulterior motives were at play, the fact that the foreign platforms were kept out of the market at all, could be viewed as the opening salvo in the present day tech war and the beginning of China's own push for decoupling.

Google's departure from the Chinese market is also a milestone event worth discussing. According to one authoritative commentator, what ultimately drove Google out of China "wasn't censorship or competition"; instead, "it was a far-reaching hacking attack known as Operation Aurora that targeted everything from Google's intellectual property to the Gmail accounts of Chinese human rights activists."[24] While the cyber espionage group Elderwood behind these attacks has never officially been linked to the Chinese government, some experts suspect that it is based in Beijing and has relations with the PLA.[25] Regardless of whether these claims are true, what many perceive to be the Chinese market's hostility to foreign companies is no new phenomenon.

[23] Charles Gibson, "China's Facebook Status: Blocked," ABC News, July 2009.

[24] Matt Sheehan, "How Google took on China—and lost," *MIT Technology Review*, December 2019.

[25] Mark Clayton, "Stealing US business secrets: Experts ID two huge cyber 'gangs' in China," *The Monitor*, September 2012.

More recent hostility between the United States and China, particularly after the Trump administration took the helm in 2016, has only exacerbated the tech war. Between additional bans, "trade sanctions, investment control, export control, and restrictions on the exchange of technological personnel" on both sides, U.S.-China relations have only deteriorated further, especially so on the tech front.[26]

In the present day, neither country's technology companies can participate fully in the other's market. As mentioned previously, the PRC government has, directly or indirectly, blocked many foreign tech companies from operating in China. In the United States, many Chinese companies occupy spots on the notorious "Entity List," which limits their ability to interact with both the U.S. market and U.S. investors. Huawei, SenseTime, and ZTE are notable names on this list. WeChat and Tik Tok almost made it to this list, though President Biden reversed those two additions after being elected into office. He did, however, update the list with 59 Chinese defense and tech companies in 2021.[27] Moreover, CFIUS—the Committee on Foreign Investment in the United States— rules enacted in 2018 prevent many Chinese companies and funds from investing in American companies on terms they view as acceptable. In sum, decoupling efforts have strengthened on both sides, and neither seems ready to reverse the trend any time soon.

INVESTMENT: A TWO-WAY STREET

As the United States reduces or shuts off most Chinese investment in its technology sector via CFIUS rule changes and other measures, it is worth remembering the key role that American investment in China's technology sector played in the sector's early development. A substantial amount of this American investment came in the form of venture capital— renowned Silicon Valley venture capital firms like Sequoia, Granite Global Ventures, and Doll Capital Management, recognizing the immense potential that lay in the Chinese technology sector, invested heavily in the

---

[26] Haiyong Sun, "U.S.-China Tech War," *China Quarterly of International Strategic Studies*, Vol. 05, No. 02, pp. 197–212, 2019.

[27] "US releases list of 59 banned Chinese defense and tech companies," Nikkei Asia, June 2021.

companies they believed to have potential. These firms created substantial China-focused funds in the mid to late 2000s.[28] Their investments, as noted earlier, helped build some of China's most impressive technology companies, including Alibaba and Baidu. Notably, these investments took place despite restrictions that, at least on paper, prevented (and continue to prevent) foreign investors from investing directly in Chinese companies conducting business in sensitive sectors—these firms instead invested in these companies through VIE (Variable Interest Entity) structures, whereby the relevant Chinese company is effectively controlled by an offshore entity, facilitating investment from overseas funds. The Chinese government historically looked the other way when these transactions occurred, likely because it appreciated the helpful role of foreign (particularly Silicon Valley) investment in building successful tech companies.

Silicon Valley VC firms provided their portfolio companies in China with more than just capital. When these funds first began investing in China's nascent technology sector in the early 2000s, there were few experienced entrepreneurs or investors in China. Silicon Valley VCs trained, or at least influenced, many of China's leading venture capitalists—the famed Sequoia China, for example, was co-founded in 2005 by Neil Shen, under the guidance of two well-known Silicon Valley venture capitalists—Michael Moritz and Doug Leone.[29] Partners also contributed by, as is typical, joining the Boards of the companies in which they invested, mentoring and teaching the founders how to run their startups efficiently and other best practices, and working to put in place first-tier corporate governance and other oversight measures—in short, they taught many Chinese companies, funds, and entrepreneurs how to "do tech."

While the details differ in each situation, this reflects a truism that VC and other investments bring a transfer of know-how and other best practices from the investor to the investee. This transfer occurs because investors typically want their investments to succeed, and they will contribute their knowledge and experience as relevant in each situation. This dynamic is independent of, and the incentives that drive it are

---

[28] "DCM Reaches $300M Close of China-Focused Venture Fund," China Money Network, March 2014.

[29] Alex Konrad, "How Neil Shen Built A Winner At Sequoia Capital China," *Forbes*, April 2014.

not themselves directly altered by, macro-level competition and geopolitics. In assessing Beijing's recent crackdown on the VIE structure that made possible so much previous Silicon Valley investment in China's tech sector (replacing its longstanding policy of looking the other way), one can discern a determination by the government that such investment is no longer as vital as in the past. Nonetheless, Beijing (and numerous provincial governments) generally retain a favorable attitude toward at least some foreign investment in its tech sector, as evidenced by various technology sectors being on the "encouraged" list for foreign investment.

Today, the companies and funds from China's innovative technology sector that want to invest in the United States in many cases have useful knowledge and experience they would share with American startups—whether it be lessons learned from surviving and thriving in China's brutally competitive tech environment, or new business models and approaches to solving problems. All of this is in addition to their cash contribution. By shutting China out of the American technology sector, American startups miss the opportunity to learn from Chinese companies, funds, and entrepreneurs.

Quite a few of my Chinese clients over the years have been investors in U.S. tech companies. And before extensive CFIUS rule changes in 2018, the U.S. market was a favored destination for them and other sources of outbound technology investment from China. In 2015, Chinese investments in U.S. tech startups alone reached $9.9 billion.[30] Fast forward to 2020, however, and total Chinese venture capital investments in all U.S. sectors capped at a significantly lower $3.2 billion, with the tech sector seeing the greatest decline in investment over those years.[31] Meanwhile, Chinese outbound technology investment to countries in Southeast Asia increased significantly during this period. Various major Chinese technology companies have expanded into ASEAN countries; in 2020, "Alibaba, ByteDance, and Tencent all set up their regional headquarters in Singapore, Huawei announced its investment in a 5G innovation center in Thailand," and "Tencent Cloud opened its first cloud computing data center in Indonesia in April" of 2021. Overall Chinese investment in ASEAN countries, already growing prior to 2021, increased by

[30] Cory Bennett and Bryan Bender, "How China acquires 'the crown jewels' of U.S. technology," *Politico*, May 2018.

[31] Thomas Haneman et al., "Two-Way Street: 2021 Update US-China Investment Trends," Rhodium Group, May 2021.

52.1% between 2020 and 2021 to a total of US$14.36 billion, again demonstrating China's shifting investment priorities.[32]

Fifteen years ago, this wouldn't have mattered to American startups, but it does now. Conversely, if fifteen years ago China had shut American investors out of its technology sector as completely as the United States is doing to China today, the China tech sector would likely not have achieved its current success.

In addition to having lots of cash available for investment, sophisticated Chinese technology companies are also important potential customers and strategic partners for the American tech sector. Often, they prefer to combine the strategic partner or customer relationship with an investment, and in many cases they even share their own ("pure") IP with the partnered startup. I've seen this happen in many of my Chinese clients' tech deals, and they typically look like the following: a large Chinese technology company invests money and licenses IP to an American startup, which co-develops an advanced semiconductor (to be owned by the U.S. startup) for (as an example) cloud computing to be sold to the Chinese company (and others) in China. This type of deal offers the prospect of enhancing the American startup's IP portfolio (by enabling it to develop an advanced semiconductor that otherwise would not have been possible on its own), increasing its revenue (by selling the advanced semiconductor product into China, a market to which it realistically would not otherwise have had access) and correspondingly growing its American employee headcount. Of course, the Chinese partner also stood to benefit via the development of the advanced semiconductor, which it could not have accomplished on its own either. Moreover, the Chinese company would often seek a Board (or at least Board observer) seat to build ties to the company in which it invested, helping the startup make key decisions (although generally, it could not alone determine the outcome) and monitoring the success of its investment.

However, now that such Chinese tech companies are severely limited in their ability, or willingness, to invest in U.S. startups, much of the appeal of creating that strategic partnership and customer relationship is lost. By the same token, if the investment is effectively precluded, or impossible on terms the Chinese company views as acceptable, the access to the Chinese company's IP that the U.S. startup might have

---

[32] Sim Tze Wei, "Southeast Asia: A hotspot for Chinese enterprises in the post-pandemic era?" Think China, May 2021.

gained through the partnership is likely also lost. All this is to say that if U.S.-China tensions continue to be the primary determinant of both countries' policies concerning technological investment and development, both governments will only be inhibiting potential growth and collaboration where they should instead be encouraging it.

The IP Environment in China

Concerns regarding China's IP theft, unfortunately often overshadowing the country's immense capacity and talent for innovation, are a principal driver of the aforementioned policies. In fairness, the concerns are not without merit. The FBI and the UK's MI5 recently issued a joint statement warning foreign companies of Chinese actors' intent to "ransack" their intellectual property.[33] Trade secret theft, software piracy, and counterfeit physical goods are just some of the ways through which Chinese actors have traditionally stolen IP. Forced technology transfers (FTT), in which a foreign business is forced to share its technology or IP in exchange for access to the Chinese market, take various forms and remain fairly common in China. FTT is also perceived to be a form of IP theft by many foreign companies—although the Chinese government asserts otherwise, as technically foreign companies still have the power to choose whether they wish to enter the Chinese market given the terms of the FTT.

In recent years, however, while intellectual property rights (IPR) continue to be an issue, the bigger story in China is innovation and IP creation. Not only has the production of counterfeits decreased substantially, but China has even become the top source of new patents globally—since as early as 2015.[34] Many of these patents concern China's tech sector. And as mentioned earlier, China has become a world leader in numerous tech sectors, from mobile payments to supercomputers and facial recognition AI software.

Mirroring China's recent success in innovation and development of IP has been its adoption of new measures to protect it. In this regard, the

---

[33] "FBI and MI5 warn that China's spies are snooping 'everywhere' with the goal of 'ransacking' companies' intellectual property," *Bloomberg*, July 2022.

[34] Ibid.

path China has been taking over the past 15 years follows the trajectories of other countries, in Asia and elsewhere, when they were at similar levels of development—namely countries protect IP once they begin to develop their own. For example, though the United States is a champion of intellectual property rights today, it too once traveled along a similar path to China's. Centuries ago, Treasury Secretary Alexander Hamilton even endorsed illicit practices such as the stealing of trade secrets.[35] It would be naive to say that this so-called thievery did not help the United States first emerge as an industrial giant.

In modern Asian history, Japan was the first to follow this blueprint. It was, as China was and still sometimes is, perceived as a product copycat, selling products nearly identical to those produced in the West. But the country also engaged in IP theft—18 Japanese business executives were charged with "conspiring to steal confidential computer information" from IBM as late as 1982.[36] Subsequently, Taiwan took the label of "perennial violator" of the USTR's Special 301 Report, as did South Korea; today, China is widely perceived as the leading "IP thief."[37]

Each of the aforementioned countries' "copycat" phases was followed by a period during which laws concerning IP protection were enacted. This "tendency of IP rights to co-evolve with innovative capacity" exists because "countries do not enact strong IP rights systems until their ability to innovate at home displaces reliance on outside knowledge."[38]

Having just started, in modern historical terms, to really innovate on its own, China is still in the early stages of building a better IP environment, though progress has already been made. Increased legal protection of IP has been a function of better laws, more even-handed application, and better enforcement. The country has set up specialized IP courts where "foreign plaintiffs actually (fare) better…than their Chinese counterparts," "increased spending on acquisition of foreign IP," developed much stronger IP laws, and upped their internal R&D expenditures.[39]

---

[35] Paul Wiseman, "In trade wars of 200 years ago, the pirates were Americans," *Associated Press*, March 2019.

[36] Jeff Gerth, "Japanese Executives Charged in IBM Theft Case," *The New York Times*, June 1982.

[37] Yukon Huang and Jeremy Smith, "China's Record on Intellectual Property Rights Is Getting Better and Better," *Foreign Policy*, October 2019.

[38] Ibid.

[39] Ibid.

China's improvements in this area have been noted by foreign entities. Members of the American Chamber of Commerce in Shanghai have
assessed that the IP environment for foreign companies in China has
generally improved in recent years, particularly compared to a decade ago,
although challenges certainly remain. Besides legal protection, other key
characteristics of the IP environment include local R&D and innovation
capability and actual level of on-the-ground IP infringement (which over
time responds to increased legal protection). Local R&D and innovation
capability is viewed by only 40% of AmCham members as a major imped-
iment, down from 49% just two years ago.[40] And while 52% of AmCham
members identified IP infringement as a concern within the operational
environment in China in 2021, this was not one of their top concerns any
longer. For reference, this number is down from 72% in the AmCham
2012 survey, when IP was a top concern.[41]

Returning to my earlier example of a typical deal between a Chinese
tech company and a U.S. startup, is there still a risk the Chinese company
might steal the American company's IP in connection with a collaboration
or at least acquire it on the cheap? Certainly, if the American startup isn't
successful, the Chinese company might have the inside track to acquire,
or at least be a likely bidder for, the IP. But at least where the Chinese
company is a major company with operations abroad and a reputation to
withhold around the world, it always struck me as unlikely it would enter
into the project with the goal or expectation of being an IP thief—and I
never saw any indication this was the case. After all, the Chinese company's goals could be satisfied without relying on misconduct or taking
on the potential reputational hit from such conduct, assuming it may
be caught were it to do so. In other words, the same kinds of disincentives that help keep companies everywhere from cheating on one's
partners in a collaboration apply to Chinese companies as well. Moreover, with the increased legal protection of IP in China discussed above,
the likelihood that any IP theft could take place without punishment
somewhere—whether in the United States or China—is reduced. Would
a Chinese company steal IP from an American startup? Possibly, but I saw
few instances of this myself. And in today's legal environment there are
significant disincentives for doing so.

---

[40] AmCham Shanghai China Business Report (2021).
[41] AmCham Shanghai China Business Reports (2012–2013, 2021).

So can foreign companies trust that their IP will be safe in China? At this stage, while improvements have been made to China's IP environment, there are certainly no guarantees. However, the path toward IP rights China has traveled thus far has been far from unique, and if as appears to be the case, it is more or less following the same historical blueprint we've seen in the United States, Japan, Taiwan, and South Korea (among others) take, then China should be on track to a better IP environment. I believe that continued progress along this path may help foster a more collaborative relationship between China and the United States, as well as other countries currently wary of China's track record.

NATIONAL SECURITY AND INTERDEPENDENCE

Both the United States and China appear to want unquestioned technology leadership and economic independence and fear their former pattern of engagement with the other risks both quests—the drivers behind decoupling. Beijing argues that Washington has started the battle for economic independence by blocking China's access to key technologies, leaving it little choice but to develop its own. But in fairness, China's push for technology leadership and independence, as evidenced by its "Indigenous Innovation" policies first launched in 2006,[42] and the rollout of "Made in China 2025" in May 2015[43] pre-dated most U.S. restrictions on China's access to U.S. technology—it has been a goal of China's leadership for some time.

Neither has achieved its objective, and both are unlikely to do so in the foreseeable future. Given the deep pool of technology talent in both the United States and China, and the significant research and development efforts taking place in both countries (and elsewhere around the world),

---

[42] "China's Indigenous Innovation Policy and its Effect on Foreign Intellectual Property Rights Holders," China Law Insight, September 2010.

[43] Made in China 2025 has been described as "a national strategic plan and industrial policy of the Chinese Communist Party (CCP) to further develop the manufacturing sector of the People's Republic of China, issued by Premier Li Keqiang and his cabinet in May 2015. As part of the Thirteenth and Fourteenth Five-year Plans, China aims to move away from being the "world's factory"—a producer of cheap low-tech goods facilitated by lower labor costs and supply chain advantages. The industrial policy aims to upgrade the manufacturing capabilities of Chinese industries, growing from labor-intensive workshops into a more technology-intensive powerhouse." See https://en.wikipedia.org/wiki/Made_in_China_2025.

it is almost impossible for either country to develop and dominate "best of class" technologies across the board. Will refusal to use—or allow the use of—one country's technologies consign the other to "second best" technology solutions in key areas? This seems almost inevitable, and also highly undesirable from the perspective of the country stuck with second class, as well as overall economic efficiency. Each country will find itself in this position in some technology areas if current trends continue.

Aggressive steps taken to achieve these goals, or deny them to the other, risk conflict. So dire is the fear of the other country dominating the "commanding heights" of key technologies and the impact of being refused access to certain best-of-class technologies on the affected country's economic performance—and as noted, each country will find itself in this position in certain areas—that it risks extreme counter-measures and even war. Neither country will tolerate this position over the long term or across multiple sectors.

A mismatch of economic systems exacerbates the situation. Put another way, the two countries do not "play by the same rules." China's system favors a larger government role, with significant state-owned enterprises, top-down government direction in key areas, and large-scale industrial subsidies. The Chinese government's use of industrial subsidies in particular has long been a source of contention between it and a number of Western countries. These countries contend that Beijing's subsidies create an unlevel playing field for foreign companies operating within the Chinese market, and more generally, competing with Chinese companies worldwide.[44] From a cost perspective, what these countries argue is nearly indisputable.

China's steel industry is a good example of this phenomenon. The country went from being a net importer of steel in 2000 to the world's largest producer by 2007. By 2013, China was selling steel for 25% less than United States and European steel, despite a "highly fragmented industry" with "no scale economies or technological edge."[45] These significantly lower costs, which made Chinese steel much more competitive in global markets, would not have been possible without the government's hefty subsidies. Other notable beneficiaries of subsidies

[44] Frank Tang, "China's industrial subsidies: what are they and why are they a source of tension with the West?" *South China Morning Post*, February 2022.

[45] Usha C.V. Haley and George T. Haley, "How Chinese Subsidies Changed the World," *Harvard Business Review*, April 2013.

from the Chinese government include China's top 6 solar companies, which according to various studies would have gone bankrupt without the government's aid,[46] and IT giant Huawei, which "has received as much as 75 billion dollars in subsidies from the Chinese government."[47] According to some analysts, this government support is what enables Huawei "to offer its products at prices around 30% lower than those of its rivals."[48] Disputes over whether Chinese subsidies fall within WTO guidelines may continue, but one thing is clear—the support of the Chinese government has been crucial to the success of numerous Chinese companies. By helping produce successful Chinese companies that did not exist before, they have arguably strengthened China's economy and produced a result that pure market-driven policies could not.

The United States has been trying to pressure China to change—essentially to adopt America's own system—for decades without much success, and recently the Chinese government has made it abundantly clear that it has no intention of doing so. In their view, their own system works better, as evidenced by China's extraordinary economic development, and they resent Washington's efforts to change it. In fairness, both countries have contributed greatly to the world's technological development. America's contributions may be more prominent over the past century—most major technologies developed in modern history have come from the United States, as have most of the systems comprising the current international order, and the world as a whole has benefited significantly from these. Many countries have followed America's example and sought to learn from and emulate the United States and how it has accomplished this. But for its part (in addition to its well-known ancient contributions to technology, i.e., paper making, movable type printing, gunpowder, and the compass), China's remarkable recent development and accomplishment, particularly in the technology sector, also deserve attention and may serve as a useful model to other countries in important respects.

In the case of industrial subsidies, since it appears Beijing is unwilling to change its policies and it is hard to argue that they have hurt China

---

[46] Ibid.

[47] Chuin-Wei Yap, "State Support Helped Fuel Huawei's Global Rise," *The Wall Street Journal*, December 2019.

[48] Shinya Matano, "The Impact of China's Industrial Subsidies on Companies and the Response of Japan, the United States, and the European Union," Mitsui & Co. Global Strategic Studies Institute Monthly Report, January 2021.

in an absolute sense, it may be advisable for the United States and other countries to change themselves instead, for example, by providing countervailing subsidies to their own companies, even if doing so would contradict conventional (neoclassical) economic wisdom. Indeed, it seems as though the United States may have already started to modify its behavior since the Chinese government has been unwilling to change its actions. The CHIPS and Science Act, which has been passed into law, includes subsidies for semiconductor manufacturing, research, and innovation.[49] This could greatly alter the way businesses operate and potentially mean the start of a new normal in the United States.

One could argue that the new legislation represents a form of the United States learning from China. It is hard to imagine the United States would adopt such measures but for China's own industrial subsidies. A question for the United States to consider is whether it should take a comprehensive look at China's economic model and identify areas from which the United States can draw lessons. It is well known that China has done this with respect to the United States for decades. Of course, China has a very different society and political system and has never adopted measures learned from the United States in wholesale form, rather adapting them to its own circumstances and giving them "Chinese characteristics." Certainly, the United States would want to do the same—i.e., take lessons from China and imbue them with American characteristics. However difficult for American pride, as the owner of the dominant economic model of the last 70 years or so, China's economic success warrants this type of review. Countries elsewhere—not only in Asia but also in Africa, the Middle East, Latin America, and even parts of Europe—are doing the same.

A PRESCRIPTION FOR THE UNITED STATES AND CHINA

As a technology lawyer on the ground in China for the better part of two decades, I've witnessed firsthand China's remarkable development over this period, with a catbird seat to observe the dramatic changes in the legal and technology sectors in particular. Today, China is a powerful country with an innovative and rapidly evolving technology sector–in many respects, the United States' peer. While China's rise has created

---

[49] Tang, "China's industrial subsidies"

considerable friction with the United States and other countries, especially recently, it has also produced significant opportunities and benefits for foreign companies and economies–including the United States. But now, the U.S.-China technology war has intensified to such a degree that it risks devolving into open conflict, a result that would be disastrous for both countries. To avoid this outcome, a new "code of conduct" defining relations between the countries is urgently needed, premised in principal part on mutual (1) acceptance of competition, interdependence, and different systems; (2) defining national security narrowly and reacting only when necessary to defend it; (3) engaging in regular dialogue and efforts to work together in areas of shared interests to develop trust; and (4) renouncing conflict and actions likely to induce it, absent exceptional circumstances.

Acceptance of competition means recognizing that the two countries will compete for influence and success, both politically and economically. For the United States, this means, among other steps, upgrading its human resources and competing for the best talent worldwide, and enhancing its R&D capability, infrastructure, and regulatory framework as necessary to improve its competitiveness. While interdependence is not a panacea, it reduces the risk of conflict by increasing its cost–although it also creates more potential areas of conflict. Bottom line, though, it is beneficial. Accepting interdependence requires both countries to provide reasonable market access to the other, which can involve measures to ensure reciprocity. In the legal sector, for example, the United States can condition access to its market for Chinese firms on American firms having the same access to China. Acknowledging different systems means ending efforts to require the other country to give up aspects of its own system that are different from one's own, except as necessary to achieve a narrowly defined reciprocity. A corollary is that where one country won't change (e.g., China's industrial subsidies), the other country should consider adopting aspects of that country's model that appear to work.

National security has long been an area where countries have reserved the right to take measures restricting interdependence. In recent years, both the United States and China have dramatically expanded this exception. For example, in the United States, changes to its CFIUS rules that began in 2018 have effectively largely eliminated Chinese investment in the technology sector. The risk is that expansion of the national security exception can overwhelm the baseline goal of interdependence, which is premised on reducing the risk of conflict, and undermine its benefits (e.g., the revenue, employment, and IP gains that an American startup might enjoy from a typical China investment). To avoid this outcome, the United States and China should both agree to define national security as narrowly as possible, resisting the temptation to expand it beyond military and critical infrastructure and into traditionally "economic" areas.

Throughout most of the last four decades, the United States and China have shown a willingness to work together on areas of shared interest, at least until recently. Keeping this going is more important than ever, even as the areas of shared interest appear to shrink. Regular, systemic dialogue–even if it often does not lead to tangible results–is important to keep channels of communication open and build interpersonal relationships. The drastic reduction in such dialogue that began during the Trump years and accelerated over the pandemic has heightened mistrust and increased the likelihood of conflict. The dialogue should be reemphasized and the two countries should try hard to work together on areas of shared interest (climate change is often cited as one such area; the denuclearization of North Korea may still be another).

Finally, the United States and China should agree to renounce military conflict other than in the narrowest of circumstances, as well as forswearing provocative "red line" actions impinging on acknowledged core interests. Such actions should reduce the risk of unintended conflict, which has been heightened in recent years by the untrammeled and expanding competition between the two countries. Of course, there is no guarantee that the foregoing code of conduct, if adopted, would prevent the United States and China from engaging in a disastrous war, but as an American citizen who has spent almost twenty years in China and has a reasonably deep and sophisticated understanding of both countries, I believe that at least it would stand a chance.

One of the things many Americans have trouble understanding about China is that, recent COVID-19 lockdowns notwithstanding, Chinese society experienced by most Chinese outside the political realm is free-wheeling, open, warm, and entrepreneurial. Many associate China with communism, but that word can be misleading. China is not a gray, drab Soviet police state—far from it. In Shanghai, expats used to joke that no one pays attention to what anyone else is doing. Streets are filled with cutting-edge fashion, frequent laughter, tantalizing scents, and all the typical sounds of a bustling city. People set up picnics in the park and chat with neighbors while walking their dogs, all just as we do in the United States. They enjoy their day-to-day lives, and this state of affairs leads to strong support for the Party among much of the population. The people know that as long as they don't cross the line into the political realm, they have considerable freedom. In short, the ways in which most Chinese go about their daily lives are not so different from most Americans. We share far more in common than many Americans—or Chinese, for that matter—might recognize.

My many years on the ground in China have taught me much about the country's remarkable history, culture, and people—truly one of the world's great civilizations. Like Americans, the Chinese are justifiably proud of their country and its accomplishments. After an anomalous one to two hundred years in which China was completely eclipsed by the West, it is back in full force on the international stage. Competition between the United States and China is almost inevitable under these circumstances, but for all our differences, I firmly believe we share many of the same values. My sincere hope is that we can manage our differences, learn from each other, and help bring out each other's best—rather than worst—impulses, as we compete. If my observations as a technology lawyer in China in this article can help in any small way in achieving these objectives, this chapter will have been a success.

Don S. Williams *is a partner with the international law firm of Hogan Lovells, based in Silicon Valley and Shanghai. With three decades of experience practicing law, split about evenly between China and Silicon Valley, he has advised technology companies worldwide throughout their lifecycles, from startups to mature public companies (venture financing, day-to-day corporate needs, M&A, and capital markets transactions). Over the years, Mr. Williams has represented private and public companies across many geographies and technology sectors, including Alibaba, Autodesk, and Grab Taxi. He has counseled venture capital and private equity funds, including Global Founders Capital, Ping An Global Voyager Fund, and Aramco Ventures, in connection with portfolio investments and other transactions around the globe. Mr. Williams is recognized as one of the top China-based private equity/venture capital lawyers by Chambers Asia-Pacific (each year from 2009 through 2022) and was named a "China Top 15 M&A Lawyer" by Asian Legal Business in 2019. At the American Chamber of Commerce in Shanghai, he serves on the Ethics Council and has been a regular participant in the "Doorknock" visits to Washington, D.C. to discuss US-China issues.*

Marie C. Williams *daughter of Don Williams, is a student at Cornell University. Having grown up in Shanghai, she has native fluency in Chinese and English. Ms Williams is now pursuing a major in Information Science with minors in Business and China & Asia Pacific Studies. Also at Cornell, she is a part of the Milstein Program for Technology and Humanity, a selective, cross-disciplinary program for undergraduate students. As a Milstein scholar, she seeks to explore the intersections of technology and business, particularly in relation to the United States and China.*

CHAPTER 3

Government and Governing: Observations of a Corporate Affairs Executive

Jean Liu

Government and its various departments are a part of commercial activities no matter where we are, but nowhere else in the world is the government's power and influence more evident than it is in China. It is an organic and integral part of business and daily life at the central, provincial, municipal, and even residential block level. The recent COVID-19 prevention lockdowns in Shanghai are an example of how governmental organs work and control lives at these various levels. Confusing at times, effective, nonetheless. Many cities have consolidated various departments' public services under one roof, making it more efficient for businesses to complete paperwork. Government services and functions have taken advantage of the many advances in technology, consistent with China's overall goal of becoming completely digital. Compared to even five years ago, a lot of the administrative work, such as filling out applications, business registration, and annual audits can be performed online—or *must* be

J. Liu (✉)
Chief Corporate Affairs Officer at EF Education First China. Shanghai, China
e-mail: jjean.liu@ef.com

performed online. However, it is still necessary to understand the system and spend time with real people in order to get clarity and answers.

A 30,000-Foot Perspective on China's Regulatory Environment

One could argue that China is a country where the government and governmental functions play the most significant role in politics, business, and everyday life. We have a large and complex governmental structure that seeps into the fiber of society, affecting matters huge and microscopic. The government's goal, of course, is to govern and serve the people. Businesses, particularly MNCs, need to have more than a nodding acquaintance with government oversight, and how different this is from the operations of governments where the headquarters of MNCs tend to be located.

The Chinese political power structure is roughly divided into four branches: the Communist Party, the government, the legislature (the People's Congress, with geographical and professional representatives, and the People's Political Consultative Congress, with representatives of industry and academic expertise, plus members of other political parties), and the military. Except for the military, the first three branches are represented from the central level all the way down to local residential blocks, in urban areas, and villages, in rural areas. It is a huge machine that touches every aspect of commercial activities and people's daily lives.

Contrast this political structure with those in the West where, in general, politicians, including elected officials, and civil servants have different roles and aspirations. In China, the line between civil servants and "politicians" is much more blurred. One can simply consider them one and the same. Senior officials normally started as entry-level civil servants and worked their way up to positions of power and influence. Officials, and the bureaus they work in, are measured by KPIs, just as company managers are. The difference is that KPIs set for government officials and bureaus are often inflexible, even artificial. And they change from time to time, depending on the priority du jour. When working with different levels of officials and the bureaucracies they work for, we must try and understand their KPIs. Otherwise, we will never understand why some of our requests fall on deaf ears.

Government officials get reassigned all the time. The Chinese government has excellent cadre succession planning, better and more consistent than any corporate human resources succession planning I have ever known. Civil servant talent is recruited at the entry level through formal exams and interviews. Young officials then hone their skills and political savvy through "on-the-job training." Mid to senior-level officials are rotated and reassigned as they move up the career ladder—a process that gives them a chance to work in different fields and locations and, equally important, little chance of forming cliques. Senior state-owned enterprise and university leaders are also considered government officials, and often shift back and forth between government positions and enterprise or university leadership roles.

Many officials, particularly at the senior level, have dual positions—both within the Party and in the government. Most officials, though not all, are Communist Party members. Some are members of one of the other eight recognized political parties; some do not have any political party affiliation.

> For corporate government affairs practitioners, the most important level of officials we work with are the department heads or deputy heads (chu zhang—处长). They hold critical positions in ministries, given their specific areas of expertise, and in local government, given their broad range of responsibility and power. Much of the work important to MNCs is in the hands of these department heads. They draft and interpret important regulations, review petitions, make recommendations, and grant approvals of many of the applications companies submit. There is a saying that the Chinese economy is a "chuzhang jingji," meaning a department-heads economy (处长经济). Without the department head, nothing gets done. Developing and maintaining these senior-level relationships is critical for success.

There is a misconception that China does not have a good legal structure. While legal services may be a relatively recently recognized profession in China, the country may have the most comprehensive set of laws in the world, certainly more than in most countries.

There is also an established process for the passage of new laws. In fact, this process can be quite long and democratic. In the case of laws relating to business, drafts are sent for review to various business communities, organizations, and individuals with relevant expertise. Comments are collected, summarized, and often incorporated into the next draft. But government acceptance of suggestions has its limits.

MNCs, like their Chinese counterparts, have the opportunity to review and provide input to new laws before they are finalized. This is often done through business associations, such as chambers of commerce. The American Chamber of Commerce in different cities has been an active and effective participant in such processes.

MNCs should take the opportunity to participate. Some may be skeptical and deem such opportunities a waste of time, thinking that the views of foreign business communities may not be taken seriously. Well, how would we know if we don't participate? How can we be critical of certain clauses if we do not speak up? It is worth the time and effort for those occasions where the process does work, and we are heard.

My experience has been that the more one participates in these reviews, offering productive opinions, the more one's views will be solicited. It is simply human nature to ease our burden of work; government officials are no different. They value contact with those who are responsive, thoughtful, and helpful.

Not all regulations or policies are equally important, of course. Though the language or terms used can be the same, the real meaning of each can be quite different from similar laws promulgated in the West. Take the data security and related laws passed in China in recent years as an example. While data security is about national security in China, it is often seen in the context of commercial opportunities in the U.S., and privacy in Europe.

Some industries are more sensitive than others. This is probably true everywhere, but particularly true in China. I've had the privilege, in recent years, to work in the for-profit or "non-state" education and training sector. Contrary to common assumptions, this is one of the most highly regulated industries in China. What is so sensitive about teaching languages? Language training is more broadly defined than obtaining a skill or a tool. It is part and parcel of education, and education is believed to play a critical role in influencing ideology and mindset. So, when we look at industry policies from a political lens, we can easily understand why the "harmless" language training industry is under such scrutiny.

Let me illustrate the complex and unclear nature of the regulatory environment by using the example of the relatively recent changes in the education sector and how this affects business. Since there hadn't been any comprehensive or clearly written rules for private, for-profit training businesses, such businesses tended to follow the rules governing corporations. The Ministry of Commerce (商务部) and its lower-level organizations (商务委) also played an important role in granting approvals to foreign-invested enterprises in this sector. The Market Administration and Regulations organization (市场监督管理局, formerly known as the Administration for Industry and Commerce, 工商局) issues business licenses and was responsible for regulating this sector from advertising, pricing to consumer protection, and several other areas. This industry was also a poster child of non-linear, inconsistent governing. Education authorities were not involved for the most part; certain provinces and municipalities did regard training designed for students under 18 as "schools," putting them squarely under the jurisdiction of the education authorities. Policies and regulations kept evolving over time. This industry sector went through three stages of transformation in the context of regulatory requirements.

First, when for-profit training began to emerge as a supplementary tool for kids' education, and a continued education opportunity for adults, it was the Wild West. Driven by parents' desire to push their children to achieve academic excellence, plus gain additional points in extracurricular activities (art, music, calligraphy, chess, model UN, coding, robotics, sports, etc.) to gain access to top-tier universities, private after-school training (AST) became highly profitable. The industry sector grew like wildfire.

The capital market began to take note of this phenomenal growth area. New investment, and a single-minded focus on profits and the desire to exit after a period of high growth and high margins, started to drive the sector into a frantic growth trajectory. What some of the players, particularly newer players, failed to realize was that the business of education is not built overnight. It takes experience, and a passion for education, for it to work well. Some began to fail due to over-expansion and miscalculation on the demand side. And failures of some of the players began to pose potential social issues. Consequently, the government began to take a much closer look at it.

Second, the desire to closely direct the education and training sector resulted in a series of new laws. Most noticeable was a recently revised law concerning "Non-State Education" (民办教育促进法). Development of the law was a long and laborious process. The law was revised at the end of 2018 and the implementation details were not issued until April of 2021. With a great deal of frustration and anxiety at times, industry players tried their best to comply with the new rules. Given the lack of clarity on how the new regulations should be implemented early on, provinces and cities, even different districts within the same city, started to use their own judgment and interpretations to apply the new rules. This has created a tremendous amount of compliance-related work. Operating the same business became much more costly, and, in the case of some companies, prohibitively so. In some provinces, adult continuing education and language training were also put under the jurisdiction of the education bureaus.

The education bureaus or departments are typically underfunded and overworked, and the non-state section of such departments is relatively small (not previously having to manage the private training sector). Then they were suddenly burdened with a large number of new "schools" without the benefit of additional resources. On top of that, they didn't, and still don't, understand how companies work, nor should they have to. In short, the education authorities were charged with new responsibilities outside of their core competence and experience. The outcome was a national hodgepodge of management systems. Somewhere during this transformative stage, COVID-19 began to spread, and teaching sites were closed. Companies that had earlier invested in online education had distinct advantages in coping with the downturn.

Third, speculations on further regulation of the AST sector of the industry began to circulate by early 2021. Most people, including myself, assumed that such regulation would be a continuation of the earlier effort, perhaps with some finishing touches. What followed was the *shuāng jiǎn* (双减) or "double reduction" campaign, which was designed to reduce the academic and financial burden associated with after-school training programs. No one expected the scale and the depth of the campaign. It completely changed the landscape of the industry.

Publicly-listed companies saw 90+% of their market valuation disappear overnight. Many companies shut down and hundreds of thousands became unemployed. Most, if not all, training companies reduced the scope of their business and pursued online efforts more rigorously, with some switching to e-commerce, selling non-education products with livestream. Though the focus of the "double reduction" campaign was ASTs, all sectors in the industry were affected. It is probably one of the most profound changes this industry has ever seen; it is also one of the most swiftly executed regulatory changes in recent history. And it has affected every company, large and small, foreign-invested, and domestic.

Despite all this, the for-profit education sector still has opportunities to grow and prosper. Chinese culture's emphasis on education is in our

DNA. People believe in the competitive advantage of a good education, and such education can take place outside of the traditional classroom. At the risk of sounding self-serving, I would argue that language learning, particularly English-language learning, remains important. No translation tools and apps can replace interpersonal communication through a common language. Cultural understanding and appreciation is best achieved when we can speak a common language.

Experiential learning, technology-enabled teaching, and non-traditionally defined curricula are all areas for further exploration. One of EF's most popular livestream sessions, for example, was "How to pack for travel," taught in English, at a time when COVID-19 cases had dropped and travel restrictions relaxed. Another area of potential growth, one encouraged by the government, is vocational training—adults must, and want to, continue to retool, and gain new skills to ready themselves for the changing job market.

One of the ways to determine the political implications and sensitivity of a new law and the associated set of regulations is to pay attention to the ministries which worked on them and issued them. For example, the series of data security-related laws were the product not just of the Ministry of Information Technology, but also of the public security and national security organizations. In the case of the new set of education and training-related regulations, the directives were issued by the Ministry of Education, the State Council, and the Central Office of the Party. With these levels of authority, swift execution happens—no questions can be asked, and there is no room for negotiation.

One critical point I would like to make is that working within the regulatory environment is not just about understanding and obeying laws. It is also about paying close attention to what accompanies such laws, particularly new ones: the "implementation details." These are the key.

Sometimes the implementation details do not come out for months, even years, after the new law is passed. Without the "details," one cannot really follow the new law. Accompanying the "implementation details" is a set of "regulations" or "rules" or both. This is where the rubber meets the road! Most government affairs professionals spend much of our time working to understand the "regulations." These regulations can be general or very specific, depending on the law or even the organization issuing them. Another important and tricky aspect is the "policies." Policies provide the actual direction upon which the regulations are executed.

While China's regulatory structure is large and complicated, we don't have to work with every ministry or commission to understand the entire regulatory universe. But we must know our own "solar system" and the important planets to which more attention must be paid. For foreign-invested companies, consider three groups in order to get started:

Group One: government authorities with a broad range of respon-
               sibilities for foreign-invested companies, from deter-
               mining whether a company is in a restricted industry
               sector, or an encouraged sector, or anything in-
               between, to business registration, IP protection,
               capital injections, advertising, etc. The most impor-
               tant ones that all foreign-invested companies need to
               work with are the Ministry of Commerce and the
               State Administration of Market Regulations. In addi-
               tion, there are industry specific authorities governing
               the industries you are in.

Group Two: authorities with specific areas of responsibility relevant
               to parts of your company's operations, e.g., foreign
               affairs, public security, immigration, social security and
               human resources, information technology, finance and
               tax, the EPA equivalent, health, etc.

Group Three: authorities you may not work with on day-to-day
               operational issues, but whom you need to know, and
               they you, in order to keep your fingers on the pulse
               of the central government's macroeconomic develop-
               ment and strategic directions. Examples are the Devel-
               opment and Reform Commission, the State Council's
               working groups related to your industry, and think
               tanks, such as the Development Research Center of
               the State Council and the Social Science Academy, for
               example.

Companies must maintain a productive working relationship with these organizations at all of the central, provincial, and local levels. Of course, the level of intensity differs and should vary at different times. Some of the ministries manage their work vertically, such as the Market Regulation Administration, National Security, etc. Others are largely locally managed, meaning these departments report to the particular municipality. They may not have formal dual reporting lines; they are all accountable to both their upper-level functional leaders and their local government.

In conclusion, the Chinese regulatory environment is framed by law and governed by organizations at multiple levels. It also varies according to local needs and, often, the ambitions, capabilities, and mindsets of the officials in charge. Most government officials, particularly those with responsibility for governing foreign-invested companies, are very bright and capable. Many of them are graduates of tier-one universities and can read, if not speak confidently, at least one foreign language. As they may have also studied overseas, or been posted there for several years, they have a good level of appreciation for foreign cultures and business practices.

Lessons from the Trenches

It is largely true that all politics are local. Upon entering the China market, a foreign-invested company may breathe a sigh of relief when comparing China with other large Asian countries. We tend to look at the homogeneous aspects of China: one official language, one people (Han Chinese make up 92% of the overall population[1]), one continuous civilization for thousands of years, etc.

China is also a very diverse market in terms of economic development, education level, attitudes toward foreign investment, and business culture. Most government regulations are executed at the local level, most often at the municipality or district level and, in some industries, at the sub-district level. So, "search and reapply" does not often apply; a "best practice" in one place can be a nightmare somewhere else.

Local government has the mandate to issue additional regulations. They do so according to their interpretation, and local needs, on top of central government rules. More often than not, local rules prevail. The central government tends to give local authorities enough power and "wiggle room," as long as their regulations do not directly violate, or are not more lenient than, the central government's directives. There are examples where local regulations have gone too far, to the detriment

---

[1] China Statistical Yearbook, 2021.

of business. In that case, MNC companies do need to take the matter upstairs.

Local government officials also have a lot of authority in determining how to apply different regulations. It depends on what is more important to them, at a specific point in time. And it also depends on their attitude toward foreign investment.

We once had a meeting with a local official on a minor issue concerning consumer complaints. While the issue and sum of money involved were not large, a bad precedent (for subsequent disputes) might be set if this one was not resolved amicably. The official in charge was dead set against foreign investment; he simply believed that every foreigner in his city was a spy and that foreign investment was harmful to the country. When we cited foreign investment and corporate laws to argue our points, he simply stated that he did not care about those laws. He only cared about consumer protection law and, even more, about his interpretation of that law. His interpretation was that companies should cave in to demands made by consumers, no matter how unreasonable or unlawful.

To officials like this one, foreign-invested companies represent uncharted waters, new challenges, and more work. Such companies are not seen as economic opportunities, e.g., for employment or tax revenue, as these things are not part of his KPIs. It can be rather frustrating when confronted with what we would regard as irrational judgment calls. This is where developing and maintaining friendly relationships over time makes a difference. Logic and rational reasoning would not get you anywhere.

Everyone, including fresh-off-the-boat expat executives new to China, seems to know the importance of relationships, or *guanxi*, where China is concerned. The fact is, good relationships are important everywhere. As the concept has been elevated, in some quarters, to the "end all and be all" level, let me touch on the notion of relationships.

Relationships are indeed important to getting things done in China. Good relationships get you in the door, ensure you a seat at the table, enable problem-solving, and, often, point you to the right direction. They can make a big difference.

How do we build and maintain relationships? It is a matter of time and effort, particularly time. There is no "quick win" when it comes to relationships. I am often asked, "do you know someone in X organization or Y province?" Knowing someone does not equate to having a relationship. We all know someone, somewhere. Productive relationships take time to build, and trust even more time to earn. And relationship-building has changed a lot over time.

The days of heavy drinking and lavish meals in the name of building relationships are largely over. The current "Eight Disciplinary Rules" fostering a more clean and efficient government have very specific restrictions when it comes to meals and entertainment. Officials' careers could come to an early and unpleasant end if these rules were violated. It is not a risk they want to take. People these days are also far more conscious of the health risk associated with the overconsumption of alcohol and food. Having the occasional meal together is still permitted, but it is not always the best starting point for a new business relationship.

The best way to establish a new relationship is through an introduction by a mutual friend or business associate. The most effective introductions I've had have come through another official or officials with whom I've already worked successfully. "Six degrees of separation" does work.

But going beyond the introduction takes substance—working to understand the KPIs of the official and his/her department, then trying to bring something of related value to them. Listen more than talk in your early meetings. I often remind people that we have two ears and one mouth for a reason. Listen carefully to what is being communicated, listen between the lines, and watch body language. Tell them something they want to hear, something they don't know, something of substance, something interesting.

> Many military officers get assigned to government posts after they leave the military. They may not have the domain knowledge of a particular industry, but they have a great network— buddies they served with who are assigned to civilian posts all over the country. I found working with former military officers very rewarding. They are fiercely loyal and disciplined straight shooters who are happy to introduce their friends.

Building and maintaining relationships is an investment. It should not be transactional. Americans, more than my European and Asian colleagues, seem far more impatient when it comes to relationship-building. One cannot simply "relate" when one needs help, then cast the official aside when the need is taken care of.

Chinese officials, like Chinese people generally, have long memories. They remember your good deeds and hold grudges for a long time, particularly if your company or executives once broke a promise or put them in a difficult situation.

I once worked on a project in Beijing related to investment in information technology, a project favored by the country. But we could not make any meaningful progress for weeks, with no apparent reason. A back-channel conversation revealed the truth behind the unexplained delay: one of our long-retired senior executives made a promise, decades ago, to donate a piece of hardware to support the Asian Games. We did not deliver on that promise! Everyone in the government who had anything to do with the I.T. industry knew about it. No one would touch us, as we were seen as untrustworthy.

It took the global CEO's visit to Beijing, and a dinner hosted by a well-known United Nations official, to clear the air so that we could move forward. One of the senior leaders took me aside and officially said: "you are new and not responsible for what happened. We can forget the past and turn the page." Relationships and trust take a long time to build. And one act of perceived bad faith can ruin it in a second.

At the same time, good deeds and contributions to the industry and community are remembered, often for a long time. Tax contributions, employment, and new business ventures are of course important measures in the districts or cities where the company is located. These are given. But it is the extra efforts, however small, that will make a lasting and favorable impression. These "good chips" can help reduce or erase some blemishes down the road. Challenges always loom, and problems will always arise, no matter how careful you are. Good relationships with the local government will help you through difficult times. That is why it is an investment! The return is down the road, rather than tomorrow.

Quid pro quo is part of the scene, and necessary! Even with clearly stated policies and the best intentions of all parties involved, one should not assume everything will take place as expected. Often, we must be ready to negotiate and offer concessions on timing, location, and ceremonial matters.

MNCs often ask for things: exceptional or speedier approvals, approvals without all the documents needed, all t's crossed, and i's dotted. When situations are a bit ambiguous, relationships can play a huge part in helping the company see its requests met.

Offering something to the officials involved can be very effective. I am referring not to personal favors but to assistance that helps the other party meet her or his work KPIs; sometimes it is help not directly related to the project at hand. It must be something the MNC's local management team can agree on and execute independent of the global headquarters, as out-of-the-box thinking, and quick decision-making are often essential.

I was once waiting for approval of an important subsidy and knew that the government department I was working with had a KPI to attract MNC Greater China headquarters to their city. I brokered a few meetings between other companies and the department. It was quite a bit of work, but it was worth the effort. In the end, everyone got something they needed.

People think government affairs work involves attending a lot of briefings. True. And it is also true that most of these meetings are not substantive. Participating in these meetings is nonetheless very important. The purpose is to meet officials with whom you may not otherwise get an audience easily. It is also to see and be seen. If a company's senior leader or government affairs executive rarely shows up or only attends meetings directly useful to them, they will not be invited back.

Another notion commonly associated with government affairs work is the arrangement of meetings between the company's senior executives and senior government officials. I know that some of my government affairs counterparts spend the better part of their careers arranging meetings and working on logistics and protocols and, often, meeting for the sake of meeting. These meetings can be important but are not as significant as they were in the past. When these meetings are warranted, make them count by having specific goals in mind.

I used to organize these meetings when our senior leaders visited China because neither local executives nor I could meet this level of officials otherwise. Senior executives were sometimes my door openers. Some of them knew it and did not mind. Others, let's just say that their egos would not allow them to be "used" in this manner. In these cases, a little bit of "strategic ambiguity" maybe the best way forward.

Senior executives and officials are very busy people, often with back-to-back meetings scheduled. So, be very efficient in terms of time management and briefing document preparation. My record: four meetings and two meals in all four autonomous cities on the same day. All briefings were done on flights and or in the car. I was also very lucky to be working with a CEO who was experienced, effective, and very easygoing. Don't try this unless your CEO and his/her entourage are capable of such intensity. The last thing you need is for your senior leaders to walk into a meeting unprepared and ill-tempered.

A thoughtful and well-planned corporate social responsibility program is crucial to good government relations. It is not only the right thing to do; it is an essential part of good business. Such programs need to be sustainable over time; they need to be in sync with the government's priorities, whether these involve environmental protection, revitalization of rural areas, or combating under-employment. Pick one that your company can make a meaningful contribution to and stick with it. A national campaign supplemented with local initiatives works best. A good example is EF's award-winning rural area English teachers' training program. It has been going strong for five years. It never stopped, even during the pandemic. In fact, it grew in scope over the last two years. It is so much in line with the government's eLearning drive that it opened doors for us in provinces and cities where we would never have otherwise had the opportunity to make an impact.

Good government relations work is more art than science. It needs to fit the company's business strategies and goals. Its mission changes over time and the practitioners' profile changes as well. Professionals in this field have gone from simply the children of senior officials, with access to their parents and parents' friends, to a discipline whose scope spans policy interpretation, relationship-building, compliance, and risk management. It is and must be viewed as a critical part of the overall management of any business in China.

> We often believe that anything is possible in China. There is this notion that if we are not getting what we want, it must be because our relationship is not good enough. Or we did not dine and wine with the right people. These beliefs are very outdated. There are many reasons why we may not be able to achieve our goals or not achieve them fast enough. Sometimes, we just do not meet the necessary requirements. It has nothing to do with excessive wining and dining. We also must adhere to our own and our companies' values and ethical standards. Doing the right thing all the time gives us peace of mind and long-term benefits.

Suggestions for Policymakers

In a 2021 AmCham Shanghai survey, 71.2% of respondents listed U.S.-China geopolitics as the area of most concern for their business in China.[2] Success for U.S. companies in China, and for Chinese companies in the U.S., will lead to greater prosperity for these companies and a stronger economy in each nation. There is massive potential for growth as both expand the digital economy, where service-industry talent and innovation play an increasingly important role. Interdependence is not only necessary; it is also preferred. No modern economy can prosper without being connected with others. Decoupling, even limited to certain sectors, simply won't work. In order to depend on each other, there needs to be a level of trust; and trust starts with communication.

Effective and productive dialogues are absolutely essential. Rather than throwing rhetoric at each other (mostly to satisfy domestic political agendas), real communication needs to take place. Public use of such terms as "the China threat," "students and scholars as spies," "totalitarian," "surveillance state," etc., or "China Initiative", "Taiwan provocations," or suspending strategic dialogues on matters which affect the entire world, are counterproductive.

Messages designed for and aimed at American voters get picked up and go viral inside China. These messages have significantly undermined American soft power and credibility. They are damaging the brand appeal of American businesses. Understandably, netizens' emotions, and sometimes misguided nationalistic sentiment, need to be calmed, particularly in an election year, but decisions involving geopolitical issues should not be swayed by social media chatters. Valuable communication needs to take place via sophisticated diplomatic skills and taking cultural context into consideration. There must be enough room left for both sides to maneuver, to step back and find alternatives. While open hostility may temporarily serve the PR purposes of both sides, strong language should be used only behind closed doors.

There are so many areas we can collaborate on for the benefit of each other and the world—disease control, climate change, and green energy, to name a few. American and Chinese leadership are vital in order to create solutions that will benefit humanity as a whole. Let's put more energy into

---

[2] China Business Report 2021, AmCham Shanghai.

what we can agree on, as opposed to focusing on waging wars with one another, be they wars of technology, tariffs, or otherwise.

No matter how tense political, economic, or diplomatic relations get, we must not lose sight of our most valuable assets—the people of our two great nations. Both countries should continue to open their borders so that exchanges through education, sports, arts and culture, and tourism can flourish in a post-COVID-19 world. Such exchanges offer valuable ways to keep us connected at the human level, building goodwill, and promoting mutual, people-to-people understanding.

As I work in the cultural exchange and language training sector, I would like to illustrate this suggestion with some statistics. According to the *Open Doors 2021 Report on International Educational Exchange*, released in November 2021, more than 317,000 Chinese students enrolled in U.S. institutions in 2020/2021.[3] Though this was a smaller number than the previous year (possibly due to the pandemic and the less welcoming political atmosphere), China is still the single largest source of international students for the U.S. What better way to build soft power and promote cultural understanding?

The number of students from the U.S. studying in China has always lagged behind the number going the other way, but the number has been trending down in recent years. The strict pandemic management measures in China have severely affected not only the number of students and tourists traveling to China, but also those American companies seeking to attract and maintain foreign talent.

China, as the second largest economy in the world, wants to play a major role on the global stage, and it should. How it handles its relationship with the largest economy in the world needs to be perceived as good for the people of both countries and the world. Policies that affect the business community need to be as transparent, consistent, and unilaterally executed throughout the country. Policymakers on both sides also need to have the confidence that foreign investment will create a win–win solution for both countries' businesses and citizens. Investors' home-country influence will not easily shift the beliefs and values Chinese people have developed over thousands of years. While holding on to our principles and protecting our core interests, let's not disengage and hurl insults at each other.

---

[3] https://opendoorsdata.org/annual-release/u-s-study-abroad.

Working effectively with the government is essential for the success of MNC businesses in China. And people-to-people exchanges must survive and rise above political turmoil. If the reader has absorbed these two messages, I will have succeeded with this chapter.

Jean Liu *is the Chief Corporate Affairs Officer with EF, Education First in China. She also worked in IT, telecommunications, advertising, and the public relations sector. Her career has spanned the globe from North America to Asia, in positions including government affairs, marketing, brand management, M&A, and business development. Born in Beijing, Ms. Liu was one of the earliest Chinese students to study in the United States as an undergraduate, completing her studies at Wellesley College. She was also one of the few Chinese students at that time who chose to pursue an MBA, which she did at the University of Chicago, rather than a degree in the hard sciences. After several years working in Detroit for the rapidly growing advertising agency, DMB&B, Ms. Liu was transferred to Hong Kong, becoming the only Mandarin speaker in that office. She was also among the earliest "returnees" to China. She has been both a witness to, and an active participant in, China's economic miracle over the past 30 years.*

CHAPTER 4

China's Industrial Businesses: Decisions, Missteps, and Lessons Learned

Chun Hung (Kenneth) Yu

In 1980, I started doing business with China, working out of 3M's office in Hong Kong. Those were the days when there were few cars on the streets in Shanghai and Beijing, and most people were still wearing gray or green "Mao suits." Women who permed their hair were considered ultramodern. Although I have held over a dozen jobs at 3M, most of my assignments had linkages to China. Each time I went back I noticed that my surroundings had changed even more than on my previous visit. The speed and magnitude by which the country has evolved in recent decades are unparalleled in human history. Dramatic changes happened not only in the business world but in nearly all aspects of life.

C. H. (Kenneth) Yu (✉)
Former Vice President, 3M Greater China. Shanghai, China
e-mail: kennethchyu8@gmail.com

© The Author(s), under exclusive license to Springer Nature
Singapore Pte Ltd. 2023
K. D. Gibbs (ed.), *Selling to China*,
https://doi.org/10.1007/978-981-99-1953-6_4

Everything You Thought You Knew About China Has Changed

What makes the Chinese so encouraging and embracing of change? In my experience and interaction with the country, dealing with challenges by overcoming them instead of just mitigating, circumventing, or co-existing with them forms the very foundation of their DNA. For example, the Chinese would rather dig a tunnel to access the other side of a mountain than build a winding road around it, even though it's more difficult. Building dykes to overcome floods is a band-aid solution. The efficient solution is to divert the flow of the flood by creating tributaries. When there was no available floating hoist in the world that could lift the submarine concrete channels for the Hong Kong, Zhuhai, and Macau Connection, instead of changing the design of the optimal submarine concrete channel, the Chinese built a new floating hoist to do the job. These, and the nation's highway and high-speed train networks to support the vast population's needs, are well known. The conversion of desert into forest and farmlands and the building of a railway over permafrost at an altitude of over 5,000 meters from Golmud to Lhasa on the Tibet Plateau is less publicized. The common element in all these efforts is the determined need for long-term and persistent results despite obvious short-term unprofitable returns.

Chinese philosophy describes this as *kǔ zài dāngdài, gōng zài qiānqiū* (苦在当代, 功在千秋), meaning "while the burden is imposed on the current generation, the benefits are to be enjoyed by generations to come." The Chinese are willing to suffer short-term pain if they foresee positive results in the future. Overcoming them has become a way of life. While history tells us about the past, it also projects the future. Yet, we need to catch up with the changes because the projection of the future may not be fast enough for China.

What Has 3M Done to Stay Ahead of the Changes?

Coping with changes is good, but taking a lead is better. I will cover how 3M did that in the latter part of this chapter. Let me first share with you what I see as one of the best strategies that 3M has deployed to cope with the rapid changes in China in the early days—the development and retention of local talent and leadership. This is not easy.

The young generation in China knows they will have good opportunities. To get ahead of the game, knowledge is what they would look for besides compensation. They see the opportunity to learn as a vital part of their career development.

At the turn of the century, many foreign companies had already discovered business opportunities in China and, therefore, invested in building their operations and hiring people. Leadership positions were mostly filed by foreign service employees (FSEs) brought over from the parent company. Undoubtedly, the corporate culture can be ensured, but the language and cultural barrier did not help. Worse yet, the lack of enthusiasm to train the locals make progress difficult.

To succeed in China, or anywhere else for that matter, we need to train, develop, and retain talents. This is how 3M has done well practically everywhere. Apart from providing vocational training locally in China, 3M China routinely had five to ten people undergoing three to six months of training in the headquarters in St. Paul, Minnesota, or centers of excellence in other countries. The rotation never stopped. As the company expanded, more job promotion opportunities were created. In the meantime, 3M China kept the compensation level distinctively higher than most peer companies. For those who needed to contact customers and suppliers on sites such as the sales, technical service, and sourcing personnel, we helped them buy their cars by funding 70% of the purchase price in exchange for their permission to use the car 70% for business. These employees own their cars from the outset.

Of course, all these cost money. One time I was asked by one of my peers in another foreign company. He asks why we would spend so much money on the people. He said if they become better, they could leave. I answered with a question: what if we do not spend the money to make them better and they stay?

Is Investing in China Still a Smart Thing to Do?

President Donald Trump thought it was. At the signing ceremony in Beijing on November 9, 2017, and with President Donald Trump and President Xi Jinping presiding, the two countries signed a number of commercial deals amounting to over US$250 billion. One of the deals was the formation of the China-U.S. Industrial Cooperation Partnership Fund between Goldman Sachs and China Investment Corporation (CIC) which is China's sovereign wealth fund. The idea was to invest in U.S.

companies in manufacturing, consumer, and healthcare businesses that either have or can further develop their businesses in China.

We know the relationship between the two countries has changed dramatically after President Trump's 2017 state visit to China. However, we must not forget the investment spree had been going on for decades, albeit with some ups and downs. Early investors who started as early as the 80s may have already collected their payoffs, but more is yet to come. Many of their operations in China are their biggest subsidiaries in the world. Undoubtedly, would-be investors are questioning their timing, privacy, intellectual property protection, and repatriation of profits. On top of these, the current Sino-American trade relationship is indeed problematic. Regardless of these issues, there are still big U.S. companies cashing out.

To do well in China, one has to know and understand modern China, and watching the news on TV and social media alone is insufficient. Investors must treat China as a business partner and understand its needs and wants. One of the high-profile examples is Tesla.

In July 2018, under the intense heat of Sino-American trade conflicts, Tesla signed an agreement with the Chinese authorities to build a mega plant in Shanghai with a clear understanding that Tesla China would be 100% foreign-owned, a very first in the auto industry in China. The building was finished under one year, and production started two months thereafter. The rest is history. What has Tesla done right? Tesla understood China's determination to switch from fossil fuel to renewable energy. It is not just being nice to the environment. It is national energy security. Tesla started proposing the idea to Beijing as early as 2015. They also took full advantage of the Sino-American trade conflict and came out as the white knight as far as the Chinese were concerned. I believe all these have helped Tesla secure 100% foreign ownership, lightning speed in plant construction, and the opportunity for clear domination of the Chinese electric vehicle (EV) market. To put the icing on the cake, Tesla China also makes China one of the biggest exporters of EVs. This means improving GDP, gaining foreign exchange, and the good name of being a good global citizen in combating climate change. All these are China's top priorities.

As new market opportunities emerge, it is by no means given that foreign companies will capture them. Seeing the country's strategic move toward EVs, Contemporary Amperex Technology Co. Limited (CATL), a Ningde, Fujian-based manufacturer of batteries for EVs founded in 2011 started going after domestic EV OEMs. By mid-2021, it was running neck and neck with the world's leader in this business at the time, LG Energy Solution of Korea. Between the two, they shared over 50% of the world's market for EV batteries. The same year, CATL opened its first overseas manufacturing operation in Erfurt, Germany. CATL has done many things right. They identified the opportunities early and made a commitment to capturing them early.

On July 1, 2022, three Chinese airlines jointly announced orders for 292 airplanes, the A320neo from Airbus, in the midst of the frigid Sino-American relationship. Deliveries will extend through 2027. Few would argue that the timing of the announcement by the Chinese was not politically motivated. However, I must point out that most, if not all of these 292 A320s will be manufactured in Tianjin, China. Airbus opened its Tianjin assembly plant in 2008 and delivered the first A320 in 2009. As production escalated and experience gained, the Tianjin assembly site eventually turned into a full-service A320 Delivery Center. By now, they have already delivered over 500 A320s of various versions to Chinese airlines. Depending on which study you are looking at, China is projected to need 6,000 to 8,000 new aircraft over the next 10 years. All of a sudden 292 A320s don't look like such a big number. Had it not been because of the COVID-19 pandemic, China would need to buy more than what they had just ordered. Airbus did not win these recent orders because of the current Sino-American scuffling. Airbus won these orders and the previous 500 A320s because they had the foresight to manufacture the aircraft in China.

Reasons not to Invest in China

The size of China's consumer market is not a good enough reason alone to invest. Successful experience usually helps, but it also makes one more prone to planning fallacy and optimism bias. Unless you have a thorough understanding of what China and the Chinese people and businesses need and want, knee-jerk investments in China tend to yield only lackluster results at best. Your competitors' success in China is not and should not be considered a promise for positive returns. Believing your colleague or a friend knows someone in the government who will make things easy for you is a dangerous bet. Halfhearted window-dressing investment in China may make your annual report look good the first year, but the lack of measurable results the years after will come back and haunt you.

Depending on what business you are in, the current political anti-China sentiment may become a headwind for you.

Furthermore, industries that require any of the three "Bad Highs" are not welcome even if they were early entrants and had been doing well during their early days. The three Bad Highs are high pollution, high power consumption, and high water consumption. At one time, Bitcoin mining was a big industry in Inner Mongolia, where electricity was cheap. Due to excessively high electricity consumption, Bitcoin mining was officially banned in 2021. By now, all of them have already left. In the early 1980s, tanneries were among the most welcome early entrants to Dongguan, a city near Guangzhou, because they hired many people and helped earn foreign exchange through their exports. They were also among the first to move out in the late 90s as the pollution control standard was elevated. The cost of water used by industries has also increased.

WHY INVEST NOW?

While there are many definitions for middle-class income, I use purchasing power as the yardstick to infer that China has a middle-income class as big as the population of the entire United States. If that is not enough, China has lifted 800 million people out of poverty since 1990, according to the World Bank. This also explains that China's economic growth is no longer concentrated in the top-tier cities of Shanghai, Beijing, Guangzhou, and Shenzhen.

For example, in the early 2010s, the world's photovoltaic industry was centered in Hefei, Anhui, a province that was hardly heard of in the western world despite being adjacent to Shanghai. In about a decade, the significant capacity building took place in the western provinces. China has also been building a large number of solar farms in this region.

The strength of the supply chains in China for virtually everything they make (with a few exceptions) for both domestic consumption and exports is not news to most people and readers of this book. The challenges to China's supply chains in recent years have only proven its resilience and superiority.

While domestic consumption is increasing, investors often overlook the high value-added exports of China-made products that are consumed outside China. This includes not just established exports such as household appliances, ceiling fans, lighting, bicycles, and toys. No doubt these are profitable businesses, but there are already stakeholders doing well.

Here, I am specifically talking about new exports that are still growing at an exponential speed. There is still room for new players who can contribute to improving the business through technology. These are also businesses in which China takes a disproportionally high global share. Examples include tunnel boring machines, gantry cranes at container terminals, shipyard cranes, high-speed and subway trains, construction equipment, electric buses, automobile parts, microchips down to 28 nanometers (for now), anything that can enhance autonomous driving and electric vehicles. And the list goes on. I cannot see why anyone would doubt business opportunities in China for the foreseeable future.

The Impact of Current Sino-American Relations

The Story of The Three Kingdoms (a historical description of warfare between states in China during the Zhou Dynasty, 220 to 280 AD) gives us a useful lesson for the situation we are now in. According to the book, "after being together for some time, the international relationship tends to break apart. After the relationship has broken apart for some time, countries will rejoin each other again." History has repeated itself time and again. Just look at how countries relate to each other before, during, and after the two world wars. I truly believe that policymakers in all countries are trying to do what they think is the best for their populace. On the other hand, I am also sure they understand there is no winner in any conflict, military, cultural, financial, technology, resource sharing, etc. Another analogy is pandemics. Even the worst one will eventually go away, and life will get back to normal and continue to prosper. It is only a matter of time.

With investment in China, or anywhere for that matter, one needs to understand why they can win, how long it will take, what the risks are, and how to overcome them. Simply put, you need a clear vision of what you are going into, a clear road map to follow, and the right people to execute. Now, let's look at the pieces.

Getting Serious About It

In recent decades, executives have often been pressured by shareholders to invest in China because of growth opportunities. It is essential that the CEO and the board know what the opportunities and challenges are before making or adding to investments. Most questions to ask are not rocket science, but true and honest answers to yourselves are crucial to what you would do next. So let's talk about some of the key issues to consider.

First and foremost, if your business answers the needs and wants of the Chinese populace and the Chinese government, you will have a high probability of success. We can talk a lot about the philosophical goals of the country. By the end of the day, it boils down to national security and the continued well-being of its populace. The former can be expanded into military might, intelligence security, energy security, food security, and territorial integrity. The latter focuses on the improvement of the quality of life of Chinese people at all levels which means improving the economy, more money in the pocket, driving up the GDP, building infrastructure, and better health care. China has done very well in some of these areas but others still have room for improvement.

It does not mean all successful businesses cover all these aspects, but the more your business does, the higher the probability of profitability and sustainability. Truly understanding and delivering what customers need and want is relatively easy for most established businesses. An in-depth and systematic market study is a good place to start. The Holy Grail is to create the customers' needs and provide the product to serve them before they even realize they had the need. Obvious examples are smartphones, shared-ride car services, digital payments, and online purchases with fast deliveries of virtually anything. Life was OK before them. Life has become better with them now. Let me share with you several stories 3M has encountered on how to solve customers' problems before they were even aware of them.

In the early 1990s, 3M's business in China was growing fast. We needed to expand. We had to move our China headquarters in Shanghai to a new location in the business district of Nanjing Road, Puxi. One day our Shanghai office manager told me he had a problem. He could not set up the switchboard of the office. The problem was there were not enough telephone lines in the city. Although I thought it was unbelievable not to have enough telephone lines in the business district in Shanghai almost 15 years after Deng Xiaoping implemented the famous economic reforms in Shenzhen in December 1978, I also saw opportunities. Our team knew Beijing would not want to tell investors from overseas that they could not install telephones in their offices and factories in Shanghai.

3M was never a supplier of switching equipment for the switching centers. 3M's telecom division had the best technology at the time to join underground trunk lines, which typically had 3,600 pairs of copper wires in them. This was before fiber optic. These trunk lines are typically 10 cm in diameter with 3,600 pairs of insulated copper wires in them. They could only make up to 100 meters long because of their weight. This means they have to be spliced every 100 meters. Imagine the mammoth undertaking of splicing 7,200 copper wires and insulating them one by one and doing it once every 100 meters. It took two skillful laborers at least 5 days just to do one splice. The 3M MSS (Multiple Splicing System) allowed any regular engineer to splice the 3,600 pairs in less than one day with a gas-tight (very reliable) connection. Manufacturing the multiple connector modules to do this job immediately became the top priority in 3M China. Local manufacturing started in about 18 months. 3M enjoyed a good market share, and 3M China's telecom division became the number one telecom division in the 3M world, the United States included.

As investors ourselves, we knew China needed a better telephone system. What else would industrial investors need? The country needed to step up its electricity production to feed the factories and roads to let suppliers' heavy cargo trucks bring in raw materials and exporters send finished goods to the container terminals. 3M does not build power plants, but we provide a comprehensive choice of accessories for power transmission from the power substations to the factories, offices, and homes. 3M does not build roads, but we make reflective materials for road signs that are still the standard on national freeways and provincial highways not only in China but also in most of the other countries in the world. The common denominators between the aforementioned three businesses were seizing the opportunities before the customers asked us and starting local manufacturing to improve supply chain and cost.

Understanding customers' needs and wants is important. Understanding the government's priority is like icing on the cake. If you can position your investment as those that would help the government achieve its macro objectives, you will have a tailwind helping you all along. The story about Tesla mentioned previously is a perfect example. Finding what the government needs and wants would take a bit more insight but is not impossible. Some are obvious if one knows where to look, and others are published in the public domain. For example, apart from national security and territorial integrity in the news, energy security and the well-being of its populace are always on top of the agenda. Environmental protection and reduction of carbon footprint are other well-publicized goals. More details are also readily available if you take the time to read the various Chinese government websites. It would help further if you could consult your peers who have already been in China for a few years.

WHAT DOES *GUANXI* REALLY MEAN IN MODERN-DAY CHINA?

The term *guānxì* (关系), meaning relationships, is often misunderstood. What it means in modern-day China is a good *business* relationship. The days of wining and dining and lavish entertainment are gone. If a government official or a potential business partner is so important that you need to get to know them better, I would often have a business lunch starting at noon. A business lunch meeting in the middle of the day projects a professional image. Even a nice lunch cannot be overly lavish. Typically, alcoholic beverages are not served other than maybe a beer or a glass of wine. Furthermore, no entertainer could fit in such a setting. Best of all, even a long lunch would not last more than 2 hours because everyone has to get back to work. Unless, it is a corporate-sponsored tournament which would be a very big event, an individual game of golf between supplier and customer is often an excuse for employees on both sides to use the company's money under the pretext of supplier/customer entertainment. If I were a good golfer, I would not want to play with my supplier. With a handicap of 10 per hole, I would not want to humiliate myself in front of them, either.

Let me share with you an example of how 3M built a long-term good relationship with China. Before Deng Xiaoping announced the reforms to open up the economy, 3M had already established a business unit in Zug, Switzerland, and started cultivating business relationships with the "unknown" China. The leader, a good friend of mine, Mr. John Marshall was the key link between 3M and the Chinese government. John visited China, mainly Beijing and Shanghai, an average of 3 times a year. John's mission was to inform the bureaucrats about 3M's values, technologies, global coverage, and the track record of developing a win-win relationship with the host government. He was like a missionary preaching the 3M story. As the opening up of the economy started, 3M started doing its business.

Due to the close proximity and language skills, a few individuals in 3M Hong Kong, myself included, were selected to work with China Trade on a shared-time basis. Incidentally, that is when I started working in

China in February 1980. Apart from doing business with China out of 3M Hong Kong, John continued his mission in China the John Marshall way. While business with China continued, one day in mid-1984, 3M announced the opening of a wholly-owned subsidiary in China, head-quartered in Shanghai. This is the first wholly foreign-owned company in China the government has ever approved. John told me knowing 3M was such a diversified technology company, the government also gave 3M special permission to import any 3M products for market evaluation purposes before 3M would decide what to manufacture. Exactly, how John did it I still do not know. I know his patience, persistence, and sincerity have earned the trust and appreciation of the people he nego-tiated with. John is an Englishman. He does not smoke. He drinks very little socially. He does have an excellent sense of humor.

Pack Your Own Parachute

If you already have an established business in China, doing due diligence will be relatively easy. A conventional due diligence process overseen by the local leadership reporting to someone who can talk to the CEO would be a good start. Inputs from China CEOs of peer companies are also helpful.

For newcomers, just like when you first started your company or when you made an acquisition, you know better due diligence leads to better decisions. Investing in China is no different. Somehow we often tend to think doing due diligence in China is easier because there are many service providers claiming they can help you. Companies often pay a high price for such services and support the service provider with a few of their own mid-level employees as coordinators. An executive often leads on a part-time basis. Such an arrangement will most likely lead one to a situation where they learn exactly what they wished to hear, not necessarily what they need to hear.

It is fine to use a service provider. To do it right, you must have your own team go to China and live there weeks before and after the due dili-gence. If the leader is not at the corporate level reporting directly to the CEO, he or she should be at least reporting to an executive who reports to the CEO. Better yet, he or she should be someone the CEO knows and wants to groom as one of the leaders of the company in the future. Successful multinational companies in China often have their CEOs and their direct reports visit China regularly. Global business leaders do it multiple times annually. After all, China is an important part of their portfolio that they cannot afford to neglect.

LISTEN TO YOUR CUSTOMERS, ESPECIALLY TO THOSE YOU LOST

During due diligence, apart from internal studies, it is essential to meet people who do business with your company, both buying, and selling. Usually, we do a good job verifying suppliers and service providers. Often, we forget the people who are most important to meet are the customers and the reasons you want to meet them. It is OK to be open and frank. They know why you want to see them. If you already have an established business, this is also the time to find out more about how your company is doing. The motto is: "if you want to know more about your own company, ask the customer." Sometimes you may be surprised.

Visiting your biggest customers should be a priority. Those visits would not take too much of your time. A business lunch with your key people and theirs in a small group of, say six, is probably the best. The key customers you probably want to see and learn from are those who've been engaging with your business significantly less in recent times and those with excessively overdue accounts. These are the people who can tell you not only what you like to hear, but also what you need to know.

Most Chinese, especially those over fifty, tend to be overly polite, especially to foreigners. Chances are they would feel the need to sugarcoat everything they say. Making guests happy is considered a form of courtesy, especially to foreigners. They generally would not volunteer the negative aspects of your company. You need to ask your questions the right way. Instead of asking how your company can improve, ask what the customer likes most about your company. The customer will tell you all the nice things, thinking he is doing you and your people a favor. Thank him for the compliment, and then ask him to name two things he would want to see your company do better. After all these, ask him what your people need to do to help make sure he pays on time. If he had legitimate issues, deal with them. If he promises to pay punctually, thank him for giving you a "big face." Trust me, your people will see you as a hero.

The more important customers you want to see are those who dropped their purchases. Be frank and open to asking what your company has done wrong or if competitors have done something you cannot match. When everything is said and done, ask the point-blank question of how your company can earn back the business.

WORKING WITH GOVERNMENT OFFICIALS

First, you need to understand the dual-title system in China, viz., the official titles, and the party titles. The official title typically describes the job of the person. The party title designates the level and power in the party. Sometimes a person may carry more than one title, it is the party title that bestows the power. For example, Mr. Xi Jinping is the President of China and Party Secretary of the Chinese Communist Party. It is the latter that carries the power when it comes to internal and external affairs and all key decision-making.

Chinese officials often (but not always) have multiple deputies. For example, a city mayor typically has multiple vice mayors responsible for different areas. For business discussion in a major city such as Shanghai and Shenzhen, unless it is a mega deal, typically, you would be dealing with a vice mayor. The mayor will appear toward the end of the deal-making for ceremonial purposes and to assure the business partner that they are well-versed with the deal and supports it. In second and third-tier cities, the mayor might be the key contact right from the beginning. If you deal with a mayor who is also the party secretary, you have the best contact you can get.

Chinese take the Orders of Precedence (social protocols) very seriously. For example, If Joe Biden visits China, he will be received and hosted by Xi Jinping. If Kamala Harris leads a delegation to visit Beijing, she will be received and hosted by Wang Qishan, the vice president of China. When it comes to major events, every detail is meticulously mapped out in advance. These include exchanging business cards, who sits where, who starts the meeting, what to talk about, etc. You want to find out the names, titles, and portfolios of the participating officials in advance. It is fine to keep a cheat sheet with you. While WeChat is a very popular tool for maintaining contact with each other after rapport has been developed, it is always a good idea to bring plenty of business cards with you especially when this is the first time you meet the other party.

Working sessions between lower-level staff on both sides may be informal. Meetings and/or dinners involving senior executives and senior government officials are generally ceremonial but serious. The size of the conference hall with the U-shape set up with two people talking through their interpreters is a sign of respect to you. Make sure you bring your own interpreter who knows what you want to talk about. Avoid jargon, acronyms, and sports metaphors. If possible, rehearse your lines with your interpreter before the big meeting. Be sensitive to where you and your team will sit. It is OK to invite one of your lieutenants who sits just next to you to make a comment, but not too often. Don't forget to bring your own photographer. Getting the host photographer to share event photos with you after the fact is challenging. Your local Chinese senior executives should be able to advise you on such details.

In fact, the dual ladder title hierarchy is a blessing because it spells out who is in charge. The only area you need to pay special attention to is to find out the job portfolio of the vice mayor you will be meeting with. This is easy to do because it is all published on their official websites. Say you are talking about healthcare related business and the vice mayor's portfolio is healthcare. You know the government is taking you seriously. If his/her portfolio is agricultural development you would know how your business is positioned in the eyes of the bureaucrats. There is one more important detail you need to know. Unless, the mayor is present, lower-level officials, as well as your people, would routinely address the vice mayor as mayor. You should do the same. However, be sure to find it out beforehand so that you know who you are dealing with.

Chinese bureaucrats today are very well educated and promotion within the meritocracy depends heavily on track records. In the old days being an offspring of a former country leadership member would ensure a fast pass. Things have changed. Today, the Organization Department of the Central Committee of the Chinese Communist Party (*zhōngguó gòngchǎndǎng zhōngyāng wěiyuánhuì zǔzhī bù,* 中国共产党中央委员会组织部), commonly known as *zhōng zǔ bù* (中组部), practices an extremely strict and organized system of the performance appraisal for all levels of bureaucrats. Senior appointments are decided through consensus at the Central Committee or even the Politburo. Performance is gauged directly with results versus goals. Their business decisions are often related to the goals set by the People's Congress and the Party. The best way to interact with these people is to treat them as business partners. To be effective in working with the bureaucrats, the work agenda is typically set up by senior management and the leading official. The working level staff on both sides will work together in the same way as two business teams. The leaders on both sides as well as their superiors will emerge at the signing ceremony when the deal is all set and done. The senior officials have all been well briefed on the details of the deals. You can feel that in the dialogue.

SPEED AND PERFECT EXECUTION

The Western world tends to look at the incredible speed things are done as "amazing" and stop there. A few good examples include the retrofitting of a bridge (San Yuan Bridge) in Beijing's major thorough-fare in 43 hours, building a 1,000-bed hospital (Huoshenshan Hospital) in Wuhan, Hubei in 10 days fitted with complete operating room setups, negative pressure wards, wastewater treatment, and 5G communication, and building a 10-story building (Broad Living Building) in Changsha, Hunan in 28 hours and 45 minutes. Searching these names in parentheses on YouTube will give you a first-hand impression of how they were done. These videos demonstrate the speed and perfect execution of well-planned strategies. Before, any of these projects were completed there was a great deal of preparation, training, simulation, and practice, practice, practice.

This brings up an aspect of leadership that the Chinese workforce expects and respects is the ability to *jízhōng lìliàng bàn dàshì* (集中力量办大事), meaning the ability to concentrate all resources to execute big matters. Despite all the preparations, the name of the game is not just speed but also perfect execution. What this means is that you and your team have to come up with a level of leadership capable of planning and organizing that the Chinese workers would respect and appreciate. The leadership must know how different components of the execution would work and be a part of the execution team. This cannot be delegated. At the end of the day, it is perfect execution that counts. In any of the above examples, there is no room for failure. Perfect execution is the name of the game, and that is all that matters.

FUNDAMENTALS THAT NEVER CHANGE

If your business is as good as you think it is, I can assure you that you will have competitors. Some will be your global competitors that followed you to China, and others will be domestic players. The latter will be your biggest challenge. They are also your best references for how your own business can do better. Don't just fight them. Learn from them as well. There is no such thing as a silver bullet that takes care of everything. On the other hand, there are some basic principles to keep in mind.

If the prospects of your business do not seem profitable, local business people will not risk competing with you. When you see competition, you have come to the right place with the right business. I assume you already know your global competitors and how to deal with them. In the following, I am concentrating on the local competition. Generally, local competitors will imitate what you make and sell them at lower prices. Keep in mind that none of them would do this to lose money. You should have anticipated that you will encounter this and be prepared to maintain your margin through better productivity, performance, and cost reduction. You can still demand the price you charge as long as you can prove to your customers that your products justify such prices. The days when customers only shop for price are long gone.

Chinese customers today demand persistent reliability and support. Meeting performance specifications is only the first step. Sustaining and improving performance is expected because your customer's customers have the same expectation of him. Reliability is not limited to product performance but also supply chain and logistics. Running out of stock or missing the delivery deadline is unacceptable. And the ability to deal with emergencies quickly and satisfactorily will always help you cement your customer relationship. When all products perform well, the company that stays with the customer during stressful situations and helps solve their problems promptly and effectively will remain the last standing.

A Trophy for Those Who Change and Adapt

Successful business people tend to have an instinct for good business opportunities. It's almost like they can sniff them out. Most Chinese businessmen have the additional capabilities to adapt and make changes at incredible speed. One company I have immense respect for is Shenzhen, Guangdong-based BYD. The company was founded in 1995. In 10 years, they began supplying more rechargeable batteries to cell phones everywhere than the rest of the world combined. In 2002, they capitalized on the fast-growing automobile market and started making cars (with conventional internal combustion engines).

Today, BYD is one of the biggest electric car producers in the world and the undisputed leader in making electric buses. To most people's surprise, in March 2020 they started making face masks because of the ongoing COVID-19 crisis. Today, they are among the biggest producers of face masks globally. Apart from the sensitivity and acumen to invest in totally unrelated new businesses, one has to appreciate their ability to adapt and evolve. They literally started making and selling face masks from scratch in less than 100 days and subsequently excelled in challenging other global leaders who have been in the business for decades.

COMPETITION DOES NOT NEED TO BE A ZERO-SUM GAME

About a quarter of a century ago, there was no such thing as a high-speed train in China. The Chinese railroad authorities went to Japan and Europe (mainly France and Germany) asking for help, hopefully in the form of a joint development format. The foreign suppliers were probably concerned about IP protection and did not believe there would be many future business opportunities. China had to pay a high price to buy what the suppliers were willing to sell them. The Chinese decided that they needed to control their own destiny. By now, China has the fastest commercially operated high-speed trains and more high-speed tracks laid and operating than the rest of the world combined. The would-be partners could have formed an alliance with China when they were most needed. They could have generated the profit their Chinese counterparts were only too happy to share. By now, they find themselves in an inferior competitive position in the global high-speed train market that China pioneered. This indeed is a stark contrast to the Airbus story mentioned in the earlier part of this chapter. We cannot change history, but we can learn from it.

Another example comes from Tunnel Boring Machines (TBMs). From the beginning of the construction spree for high-speed rails, China needed TBMs to bore through mountains to make tunnels. At the time, the technology was in the hands of European suppliers, mainly German. China had to pay an exorbitant price to get the equipment while also accepting humiliating terms for after-sale service. History repeated itself. Today, China's demand for TBMs is so high that OEMs in the rest of the world combined cannot meet the demand. China had to rely on itself. As more TBMs were built, experience expanded, and costs were reduced. Today, China is not only the biggest market for TBMs, but it is also the biggest exporter of TBMs in the world exporting more TBMs than the rest of the world combined. Never underestimate your competition.

Due to the emphasis on infrastructure building at the turn of the century, a lot of heavy construction equipment was needed. China was able to produce most of it. High-altitude concrete pumps can move premixed concrete to a high altitude for constructing tall buildings. The world leader in concrete pumping was Putzmeister, based in Aichtal, Germany. This is the company that holds the record for pumping concrete from the ground to a 700-meter high level of the 829.8 meters tall Burj Khalifa, the tallest building in the world. In China, Putzmeister had been competing with Sany Heavy Industry which makes heavy construction equipment. In 2012, Putzmeister and Sany Heavy Industry announced their merger. The profits Putzmeister accrued in China certainly have helped increase its value proposition, which also benefited the shareholders when the company was sold.

The automobile industry has other examples. Until 2021, all OEMs had to form joint ventures with local partners. SAIC (Shanghai Automotive Industry Corporation) and Volkswagen formed the JV SAIC Volkswagen in 1984. Since then it has been growing profitably and remained a shining star in the VW global family. Apart from making VW cars, it extended its portfolio to also make and sell other brands including Audi and Skoda. In 2018, as electric vehicles were in vogue, VW started investing in electric cars. Three plant sites have been built and they are currently selling 3 models in China. It is not an overstatement to say SAIC Volkswagen is a model JV in China. Both sides win.

Chinese businesspeople believe the market in China is big enough for everyone. Building their businesses is the priority. They do not have time to engage in petty fights or go at each other's throats. Over these years, I have not seen any business dominated by one company that can wipe out all others. Nor have I seen a Sino-foreign partnership break up and become hostile competitors.

What Has China Done
with Intellectual Property Protection?

Counterfeiting was rampant in the 1980s and early 90s. Knock-offs were found not only in consumer products such as watches and handbags but also in industrial and commercial products such as automotive parts and magnetic memory products. There were reasons but not excuses for these counterfeit activities. At the time, law enforcement, prosecution, and judicial procedures were not well coordinated. Even when convicted, penalties were too lenient to create deterrence. This started to change in the mid-90s and accelerated as China joined the WTO in 2001. The most symbolic move was the high-profile demolition of the Xiu Shiu Street Market in Beijing and the Xiang Yang Market in Shanghai, both being the most infamous open markets for knock-offs. Since then, efforts to fight counterfeiters have escalated. By 2010, government departments involved in intellectual property protection were given performance quotas for the minimum number of cases they needed to process each month. These quotas were their KPIs.

China stepped up the fight against counterfeit goods for several reasons. First and foremost, the populace has become better educated and more affluent. The pressure from the outside world was indeed part of the driving force, as the accession to WTO required China to maintain certain standards to keep its membership. Finally, as more Chinese brands emerged, the protection of IP is no longer an action to meet requirements but also an action to protect the big domestic brands. As an example, there was absolutely no counterfeit or imitation of the mascot Bing Dun Dun from the 2022 Beijing Winter Olympics.

Earlier, I mentioned 3M's success in capturing China's telephone line connection market. There was an adjacent market 3M should have also captured for cross-connection cabinets. Trunk lines are big, thick cables that come from the switching centers. When they connect to offices and homes, they branch out like trees from the trunk to big branches, then to smaller branches, until finally reaching individual subscribers. To be economical and easy to connect and maintain, the technology at the time was to set up a connection box (subsequently called the cross-connection cabinet) to receive a branch from the trunk line with say, 360 pairs of wires, and connect to the terminals on one side and let the subscribers' lines connect to the other side of the panel as and when new subscribers are added. The cabinet is just a box. The technology is in the connection blocks that connect the wires from the branch line to the subscribers. 3M had a patented block that allowed an untrained installer to make a very reliable connection with a simple screwdriver.

The product was well-tested and used effectively in other developing markets, with the biggest success in Taiwan. The Chinese service providers loved the product. Everything looked good with the credibility we earned through our products to connect the trunk lines. Unfortunately, we were sued by a small local competitor for violating their patent for the connection block. We thought it was ludicrous. After all, 3M invented the product, which has been patented. Although we patented the block in many countries, we did not do it in China. The competitor did. Although we subsequently came up with a better product a year later, we lost the opportunity to get lucrative results from the first wave. This was an expensive lesson.

Now, on to the happy story. The general public in China first learned about 3M's N95 respirators (face masks) in November 2002 when SARS first broke out. As the world's biggest manufacturer and market shareholder, 3M respirators became a much sought-after commodity for personal protection. With demand outstripping supply, counterfeit products began to appear in no time. Fighting counterfeiters in those days was very difficult, just like pushing water uphill. As the government got more serious about the issue, we saw a bright light at the end of the tunnel. Since 2011 3M China had a 100% win rate for all litigation against counterfeiters. So what had we done right to deserve this?

Stopping counterfeiters required the deployment of one of the strategies in Sun Zi's book *Sun Zi bìngfǎ* (孙子兵法) or *The Art of War*. He wrote, "*shèng bīng xiān shèng érhòu qiúzhàn*" (胜兵先胜而后求战), meaning "victors win the war before starting the battle." First and foremost, the brand and designs must be patented. The brand owner should build up a good working relationship and trust with Public Security (the police), Prosecutor, Administration of Industry and Commerce (AIC), and the external legal service providers. Next is to work on the plan and action steps like a war game. The grand finale is to just do it, but the devil is in the details. Building relationships and trust require your own people's knowledge about the laws and professionalism in IP protection. Trust can only be built up over time. Keep in mind these government departments also have their own KPIs that would recognize their contribution to stopping the counterfeiters. So they are more than happy to work with your people.

By the end of the day, the success or failure in IP protection lies more in our own hands than the host government. The atmosphere, nowadays, is for IP protection. We just have to make sure we take care of all the basics and develop a good working relationship with our law enforcement colleagues.

MY ADVICE TO POLICYMAKERS

Policymakers are knowledgeable and experienced in what they do. I am not about to tell them what they already know, such as nobody wins in a trade war, or any war for that matter. When they have differences, they should discuss face to face with an open mind. Do not let the media act as their de facto representatives.

Policymakers should exercise better control and use of the media. Media tends to sensationalize issues because it attracts audience. Distorting the truth is no better than lying blatantly. Call a spade a spade the same way they would teach their own children. This is easier said than done. Biased media coverage often helps attack the other party in the short term. If reinforced by the government, things get worse. The end result is that it will deepen the hatred between people in the countries involved. Eventually, it will lead to the ultimate eventuality, and we all know what that would be.

I have another humble idea to share with the policymakers. The best way to win is to win the admiration of the people in the other country. The idea is to create the quality of life for their own populace to the point that other countries would envy. It needs to be an environment where people truly feel happy.

While the military might help create fear in others, it also promotes an arms race that eventually drains the country's coffers. Don't get me wrong. Having an appropriate level of national defense is certainly essential. Just think about putting the excess money used in the arms race into things like better education for the young, more affordable housing, lower cost health care systems, better infrastructure, and more money into every citizen's pocket.

There is a better way to balance international trade. There is no point in every country trying to be independent with all supplies on its own. Doing so will duplicate a lot of costs and waste resources. The best way to make other countries buy from you is to produce the best product with the best price value while maintaining supply chain excellence. Customers are human beings just like every one of us. They want to get the best value for their money. You get their business by being the best supplier. In the end, we all want safety, security, and quality of life.

Mr. Chun Hung (Kenneth) Yu *is a veteran of one of the world's renowned innovative companies, 3M. He joined 3M in Hong Kong in 1969. He started his international assignments in 1984 when he was appointed as the Managing Director of 3M Taiwan. His broad exposure to international started when he was appointed Director of Health Care Business in 3M Asia Pacific covering all the countries and territories in the area including major ones like Japan, Korea,*

Taiwan, Hong Kong, Australia, and New Zealand. 3M's business in China was minuscule at the time. Over 44+ years, he has completed various leadership assignments in the Asia Pacific and the home office in St. Paul, Minnesota. Most notably, Mr. Yu took over the leadership of 3M Greater China Area in 1993, leading 3M China from a modest beginning to become 3M's largest international subsidiary. Before he retired from 3M in 2014, he was already serving on the Board of MTS, a NASDAQ listed hi-tech company specializing in testing and sensing systems. In 2018, Mr. Yu was appointed as a Consultant to Goldman Sachs' China-U.S. Industrial Cooperation Partnership Fund. In the same year, he was also appointed as an Advisory Committee Member of Nottingham University Business School Ningbo.

five-minute blocks, presented in a dry, hard-sell approach because all you had to do was repeat your brand name as often as possible to get the message out there. As a result, sales went up, thus giving marketers a false sense of success.

Advertising agencies were primarily filled with Taiwanese and Southeast Asian transplants who satisfied the increased demand for talented marketing professionals. Like everything else in China, corporate promotions on both agency and client-side accelerated at hyper-speed. Because of the need for talent, it wasn't unusual for an Account Manager to move to an Account Director role after a few years, typically a ten-year progression anywhere else. Poaching became so common that big agency networks like WPP had to set up special tribunals among their agencies to police inter-agency poaching. And even today, the average international agency's annual churn rate stands at a whopping 45%. It's no wonder that ex-WPP Founder and current Chairman of S4 Capital, Sir Martin Sorrell, declared in 2014 that China's next corporate battle would be one over human talent.

Because advertising was considered a form of propaganda, the China advertising industry was initially established under the government's watchful eye in the 1990s, and foreign businesses needed to form joint ventures with local partnerships to get their advertising licenses. China had very few local advertising agencies, so foreign agencies signed partnerships with various media outlets, many of whom had no experience in the trade. Agency partner bosses tended to be mere figureheads who would come in, sit in their corner office, drink tea, and read the newspaper all day. Some foreign agencies even had Communist Party representatives, but their job was not to spread propaganda or spy, but to coordinate employee activities such as company outings. Foreign agencies generally dominated the advertising space, especially for foreign brands. However, local shops started to flourish around 2008 with the advantages of being affordable compared to the international shops that were required to provide a percentage of operational fees to the New York/London center.

The international agencies, better known as "the 4As" taken from the acronym for the Association for Accredited Advertising Agencies, were also more generous and provided the highest salary compensation, and in some cases, higher than those working on the client side. Agencies were generally known to hire the best people in the marketing business: the one-percenters in China who were open-minded, westernized, and willing to work in a loosely structured environment, free of the traditional Confucius-inspired organizational hierarchies.

Finding these remarkable talents was initially a huge challenge because early recruits had no exposure in their lives to customer service. As a result, agencies would often recruit bilingual customer service representatives from the 5-star hotels, promising significant salary bumps and hoping to advance their careers in advertising. In the early days, if you met anyone you thought fit the profile, you would immediately try to bring them in for an interview. The results of this process created a workforce that probably wasn't the most representative sample of the Chinese public. Still, this group of Westernized Chinese youth was responsible for creating ads that would encourage the public to buy stuff.

While many of the ads in the early days would resemble generic advertising from the American 1960s, we would occasionally get a chance to do a creative one that I'm confident the masses didn't understand. One advertising campaign we created for the Range Rover Evoque launch was so esoteric that it magically worked to the brand's advantage. Consumers who saw the ad in focus groups were so confused that they naturally assumed the car must be expensive. "It's like an art painting that I don't understand," replied one participant, "so it must be a very premium car."

THE 2010S: THE SPEED OF GROWTH HITS MACH 3

When the business started booming in 2010, ad agencies greatly expanded, salaries soared, and agencies started allowing employees to take luxurious company trips in exchange for their loyalty. Eager entrepreneurs set up local shops, leaving foreign agencies to set up their own businesses. Besides lower costs, local agencies had the unique advantage of having the ability to secure deals through corrupt means, offering bribes to the client's procurement leaders. That's not to say some foreign agencies played this game. Still, their organizations established checks and balances to prevent corruption, while many local agencies considered payoffs a price of doing business.

Procurement departments, especially with government joint ventures, would attempt to dismantle global agency partnerships by enforcing outrageously long payment terms to bring local agencies who were more favorable to backhanders. Agencies would even have professional payment chasers whose sole responsibility was to chase money from the clients.

Chang'an Ford, Ford's government-owned joint venture partner, maintained a policy for several years of paying their non-merchandise suppliers 12 months after work completion, despite Ford's global 60-day payment policy. Chang'an Ford claimed it followed the payment practices of other state-owned enterprises.

By 2010, China's economy had grown by 10.64%, and trade volume rose 34.7%, making it the first year the country was declared the second-largest economy in the world. Massive growth in the property sector enabled Chinese consumers to buy expensive foreign goods at a rapid pace. At the 2010 Beijing Autoshow, some wealthier car buyers even carried heavy bags of cash to the luxury auto section, walked onto an exhibition booth, and purchased cars on the spot. Only in China were actual car sales considered a key measurement of success at an auto exhibition as opposed to other countries where people just came to look and would buy later. My agency, Wunderman, served Land Rover for almost ten years, from 2005 to 2015. In 2008, Land Rover sold under 3,000 vehicles, but thanks to a surge in the consumer economy, that number surged to over 100,000 by 2014, making China the company's biggest market. Imported from Solihull in the Midlands, UK, the factory had to operate on double shifts to keep up with the demand in China.

2010 was also the same time that the country saw a massive surge in mobile commerce and social platforms, and the world of advertising in China would change forever. While the American advertising market still has a robust traditional television component, the Chinese market is now predominantly digital, with over 85% of total ad spending allocated to digital in 2021. In the early 2000s, internet penetration was minuscule, with platforms such as Kaixin and RenRen, China's early imitations of MySpace and Facebook, which were mere copies of their western counterparts.

Video platforms, such as Tudou and Youku, grew in popularity. However, their viewership was initially confined to college students viewing their PC-based portals and still did not capture the eyes of the masses. Online video provided an outlet for quality content that was missing on the terrestrial television stations, whose content continues to be tightly controlled by the government and has a reputation for lack of innovation in programming. Online video platforms survived under less scrutiny from the strict censorship authorities, who were responsible for approving all television advertisements and programming. Advertising quickly moved from website banner ads to digital video pre-rolls and in-content product placement. But the transformative moment for online video came in 2014 when China rolled out 4G mobile services, registering as many as 576 million 4G users by 2016. Unlike their western counterparts at the time, China's video platforms were designed to be experienced on 4G, and mobile video platforms grew increasingly in popularity.

Digital media spending remained a fraction of the total advertising budget because it was considered too risky of investment in driving brand awareness and pushing product sales. Western brands questioned the effectiveness of reaching audiences based on unreliable and sometimes falsified data. Early adopter brands such as L'Oreal's Lancome built large online ecosystems to connect their audiences to their growing online community platforms where Chinese girls could share their latest cosmetics tips. New car owners would go on platforms such as Sina Weibo, an integrated, supersized version of Twitter, to share their new car purchases. User-generated content in the form of sharing photos of your first-time purchased car was so popular that netizens would refer to this practice as "doing your homework."

By 2013, Weibo's subscription base reached 500 million registered accounts and 54 million daily users, mainly propelled by celebrity accounts that Weibo helped propagate star content into average user accounts. Keeping up with Weibo celebrities soon became the platform's big draw and a strategy that helped it overcome its other microblogging competitors. Weibo might have started as a Twitter knock-off, but it quickly grew into something that represented an entire online ecosystem; it expanded its platform to enable brands to house campaign microsites, complete with product imagery, descriptions, and embedded videos. Brand content was quickly shared with the Weibo ecosystem among the subscription base, creating China's first significant attempt at integrated social media. Brands no longer needed to spend a fortune to drive traffic to their websites and could rely on an existing pool of social followers to interact with their communications.

But 2015 saw a dramatic change for Weibo when the Chinese government required users to register their real names and provide their national identification numbers. Under newly elected President Xi Jinping, the government began to crack down on those online celebrities who controlled the most significant fanbase, better known as Big Vs, meaning verified accounts, because it was worried about their increasing control of public opinion. One of the more popular microbloggers, Charles Xue, a Chinese-American entrepreneur based in Beijing, was one such "Big V." Xue was widely known for sharing his ideas about corruption and political reform with his 12 million followers on the platform, but was eventually arrested and charged with visiting a prostitute, an allegation he denied. Many China watchers predicted that these actions would spell the platform's demise, but it has so far managed to survive.

Despite these actions, Weibo has done well, mainly due to its push into video streaming and live streaming as a native feature of the platform and the fact that it remained the only way for celebrities and key opinion leaders to reach a mass audience. The actual name registration requirement benefited advertisers because they could better target consumers. In this way, Weibo could be considered an open ecosystem, while its social rival WeChat, is a closed one.

Tencent's WeChat, or Weixin in Chinese, was launched in 2011 and reached 100 million users in one year, growth partly fueled by Weibo's crackdown on the Big V's because WeChat provided a private chat environment. New users quickly set up chat groups among friends, neighborhoods, and working relationships. Companies could set up their public accounts enabling brands to follow their content in a separate tab on the app. WeChat established two types of accounts that had different content distribution rules. The subscription account enabled users to receive daily messages from brands. Still, it utilized limited functionality compared to a Public Account that included more consumer data extraction capabilities and CRM functions but was limited to four monthly posts. The big game-changer came in 2014 when WeChat went head to head-with Alibaba's Alipay and launched a mobile payments system. The existing social functions in WeChat Pay enabled individuals and small businesses to exchange money freely, creating the world's most utilitarian mobile application platform. Thanks to the power of WeChat Pay and Alipay, transactions using coins and paper money were eliminated, and ATMs mostly disappeared after a few years. Wallets soon became antiques, something saved for overseas trips, because in China, one only needed to carry a phone.

WeChat Changes Everything

WeChat currently has over 1.25 billion users and is easily the most prolific lifestyle utility globally. With over 360 million people accessing their accounts daily, its ecosystem is exceptionally comprehensive and generally indispensable to the point that one could not even fathom living in China without WeChat. No parallel global application competes with its ability to connect social, commerce, and payments, all within the same platform. WeChat is a bit of WhatsApp, combined with some Facebook features, Amazon and Paypal, making it one of the most utilitarian mobile applications on the planet. And unlike Weibo, WeChat is highly private as users can only see posts and engage with users within their contacts. To see one's posts requires permission and requires users to opt-in and connect, making the social posts stream known as Moments. Since its inception, WeChat has launched new and engaging features that keep users feverishly locked to the platform. WeChat Search, for example, was launched in 2017 and is now the primary search engine for 32% of all Chinese mobile users. Mini-Programs applications within the WeChat ecosystem now reach over 400 million users daily, enabling brands to have deeper content relationships with their customer base.

The WeChat platform's brilliance is its simplicity and ability to function perfectly on a 4G mobile platform. In the early days before Mini-Programs, most brands simply hyperlinked their activities within the platform, and WeChat served more or less as a simple web browser for most functions. Users often never knew that they were actually off the WeChat platform and simply using the app as a low-end web browser.

Despite its vast reach into the daily lives of over a billion users, Tencent's WeChat makes only 15% of its revenue from paid advertising, compared to Meta's Facebook, which is 97.9% ad-supported. Tencent's critical revenue comes from its value-added services, including mobile and video games. WeChat is, for the most part, not an ideal paid advertising platform to drive awareness, especially for smaller brands that cannot afford its high advertising rates. And unlike Google or Facebook, WeChat lacks powerful algorithms that can target by location and segment audiences by interests, and it is common for brand ads to appear on screens to those who are not interested. Despite this, WeChat is relatively ad-free, especially compared to the Meta platforms that often sacrifice user experience to increase revenues.

WeChat's key strength is its customer relationship management platform, enabling brands to have a personalized relationship with their customer base. Brands can send customized messages to customers if they opt into the brand's WeChat-embedded ecosystem. Smart WeChat systems would enable brands to connect to their customers at all touchpoints and follow them through the customer journey, sending segmented push messages. WeChat quickly became the de facto loyalty platform where customers could purchase top-up cards and receive incentives for frequent purchases. Its simple functions and highly restrictive but effective user experience protocol forced developers to create applications within the platform. Brands like Tesla created an entire ecosystem in WeChat, enabling consumers to order a new Model 3, apply for a loan, book a test drive, or direct drivers to charging station locations.

Platforms like WeChat and Weibo, in addition to the Chinese e-commerce giants, Alibaba and JD.com, have effectively created a closed and firewalled ecosystem that has left many modern international agencies and consultants outside the China ecosystem, who for the most part, rely heavily on platforms such as Adobe Enterprise or Salesforce to manage much of their digital marketing automation efforts. In 2019, Salesforce formed a partnership with Alibaba to expand its footprint in China's Software as a Service (SaaS) market, but its impact has been minimal because it initially avoided investing in new tools and technology to suit the market's needs.

China was becoming more digital and social and less reliant on traditional advertising, so brands increasingly took essential services in-house to make quicker decisions on actionable insights that could immediately help impact the bottom line. If a brand needed an advertising campaign, the conventional process involved briefing a creative agency and waiting two weeks for a big foundational idea. In a real-time social ecosystem, this method of advertising development seemed outdated and ineffective, especially when actionable, live customer data was available. My agency's role quickly became less about brand strategy and more about social media execution. Senior strategy planners were soon replaced by armies of eager but low-paid fresh graduates to churn the work across multiple platforms. Advertising agencies began to lose their influence over the decisions of their client's Chief Marketing Officer.

E-COMMERCE'S GREAT LEAP FORWARD

But there was no more significant change to the marketing and advertising ecosystem than the meteoric rise of e-commerce, which Alibaba and JD.com still dominate. China is now the world's largest e-commerce market, with annual online sales totaling $672 billion, growing 35% annually. E-commerce now represents 15.9% of total retail sales and includes e-commerce marketplaces, social commerce, and platforms that enable brands to sell directly to consumers. China's largest platform, Taobao, has become more than a shopping app but has evolved into a form of entertainment, including online events, livestream events, and influencers that engage consumers within the platform without the need to go elsewhere. Combined with a massive and sophisticated ecosystem, e-commerce shopping has almost completely replaced traditional retail in many categories. Taobao has become so infectious that the average Chinese woman opens the app at least five times a day. Since its inception in 2003, Taobao has evolved from a search-based commerce platform, similar to Amazon, to a social commerce ecosystem and finally to a live commerce one. Almost every major brand store nowadays has an active livestream program operating around the clock, and it's not just sales but customer service as well. Besides live streaming, brands also post short videos and engage consumers in physical stores. In 2021 alone, 560 million people watched livestream programming.

In 2008, Alibaba launched its glitzier branded shopping mall, Tmall, to capture a higher-tier customer and appeal to premium and luxury e-commerce customers looking for authentic products. While Taobao doesn't require sellers to pay anything except a deposit, brands on Tmall must go through a Taobao Partner (TP) and pay a large deposit and service fee to the platform. TPs first started by handling the operational side of e-commerce on behalf of the brands, including warehousing and call centers. TPs often took the role of a dealer. They would purchase product inventory on behalf of the brand, taking responsibility for the sales and distribution, earning a commission on the sales. And because of this financial burden, the operational requirements needed to run an e-commerce business were often far from the 4A agencies' and consultants' scope of work, who preferred to stay upstream on the strategic side of things.

E-commerce grew exponentially between 2010 and 2015, as did the amount of data that tracked every moment of consumer behavior through the sales funnel, from awareness to purchase experience and loyalty. Brands begin to understand the power of the e-commerce channel and the ability to reach untapped millions in the lower tiers that traditional outlets could not serve. Big TPs, such as NASDAQ-listed, Baozun, began providing foundational e-commerce distribution and customer service operations but invested heavily into technology platforms that tracked and measured the relationship between platform customer engagement and product sales. Baozun effectively integrated cloud computing, big data, and AI technology to manage all aspects of the marketing and commerce relationship for over 266 brands, such as Nike, Levi's, Tiffany, IKEA, and Victoria's Secret. Baozun's marketing model and the growth of e-commerce profoundly impacted the advertising business and ushered in the era of performance marketing. Brands began to abandon traditional advertising practices of building long-term emotionally driven equity in the form of 30-second television commercials in favor of a strategy that favored quick tactics on social and e-commerce platforms that enabled brands to see immediate results.

Agencies were brought in to deliver tactical social campaigns delivering brand experiences within e-commerce platforms during important shopping festivals. Traditional advertising agencies, such as Y&R, JWT, Leo Burnett, and Saatchi & Saatchi, once housing large strategic and creative teams, saw their businesses dwindle rapidly and were forced to consolidate their teams with digital agencies within their networks.

With performance marketing, advertising became more operational and less ideas-driven. Using innovative tactics and a pile of cash would generally guarantee a healthy revenue year. Brands would later put their trust in performance marketing influencers, often referred to in China as Key Opinion Leaders (KOLs), to push sales during peak sales periods throughout the year.

Some of the most famous KOLs, such as Austin Li or Weiya, would represent hundreds of brands during an evening livestream session requiring them to present products in rapid-fire succession, sometimes allowing less than five minutes per product. Because the top KOLs were so effective at driving sales during their performances, they would ask for exclusive discounts of up to 40%, which served as a significant incentive for consumers to purchase from their sales platforms because they knew they were often getting the best deal possible for the product. Austin Li, better known as the "lipstick king," is undoubtedly the best salesman of beauty products in the country; he once sold 380 different lipstick variants over a seven-hour livestream session. Li commands a fan base of over 45 million on his daily evening livestream performances using his sassy demeanor. Li sells products in real-time during his marathon sessions that can last anywhere from six to eight hours, taking a cut for his services. But because he commands such a massive audience, many product lines can sell out in seconds. But what is the role of marketing your brand in China when a KOL like Austin Li can sell it out in minutes during one of his Livestream performances?

Performance marketing, combined with a calendar full of Black Friday-style shopping holidays, has signaled the end of traditional marketing as we know it in China. With e-commerce now representing one-fourth of China's total sales, brands now turn to tactical social campaigns to drive purchase preference, both inside and outside the Alibaba ecosystem, relying heavily on a product's functional benefits delivered through popular livestream KOLs that demand significant product discounts, as this is often the key draw for the viewers. With a quality product, solid promotional offering, and the right channel and spokesperson, brands can deliver the goods, but this remains short-term and often doesn't last beyond a single-year cycle of sales volume.

Consumers now have become so accustomed to buying on sales discounts that they rarely purchase a product at its regular price. As a result, the discounted price, sometimes as high as 40%, has become its regular price. Since brands have become addicted to quick sales volumes through tactical promotions and driving performance marketing results, the marketer's role in China has shifted primarily to a sales support function. Agencies are now briefed to create live stream, QVC-type programs for many major brands to generate immediate volume. When launching Lysol during the middle of the coronavirus pandemic in 2020, my agency created a livestream talk show meant to educate the Chinese consumer on the benefits of an aerosol disinfectant spray, a largely unknown product here. Despite an effective livestream program, the product didn't sell well during the show, mainly because the audience didn't know the brand. Despite previous alignment on a "slow burn" launch approach, the client was extremely disappointed with the results.

Despite all of these new tools and tactics, companies cannot build brands in China from one-off tactical campaigns. The role of advertising is to help create memories that are eventually triggered to satisfy specific needs at the point of purchase. Through steady and consistent spending, those memories are activated at any moment because it is impossible to predict when a consumer will be thirsty or hungry and experience a purchase moment. Within the Chinese performance marketing environment, brands achieve short-term momentum often due to a price discount. This type of marketing model is not sustainable without erosion of profitability.

China's performance marketing evolution and the impact of e-commerce had also transformed the role of advertising agencies from a brand's strategic partner when I first came to China in 2005 to one of a creative activation sweatshop that is designed to crank out social campaigns from pitch to execution in just a few weeks. Brand managers would pitch multiple agencies for single projects that would last only for a few months, then pitch again. Once, the agency's valued partners to its clients, strategic planners were turned into the front-line army of the agency pitch factory. Because the agency work was project-based and not strategic, it quickly fell to the junior brand managers to manage agency relationships. At the same time, senior marketers rarely got involved in the process. With so many competing agencies for projects, profit margins for agencies were kept razor-thin. Making significant profits was enormously challenging, especially when competing against local shops that didn't have to pay regional and global overhead costs that were standard practice for China-based international agencies.

Welcome to the Super App Jungle

Chinese consumers are ever eager to accept new digital environments, adding even more layers of complexity with the launch of even more platforms, including Bytedance's Douyin, which later launched its global counterpart, TikTok. Food delivery platform, Meituan and social trends app Xiao Hong Shu or Red also gained in popularity. For brands, China's marketing ecosystem and managing campaigns became extremely complex. Normally, traditional digital transformation practices encourage marketers to drive their database into a single view of the customer, enabling brands to follow their customers from one online platform to the next, from online experiences to offline. But with multiple independent social and commerce ecosystems, each having nuances, many international brands, including Estee Lauder, operate data platforms separately. Chinese platforms operate on a closed, integrated ecosystem model that enables users to engage in many transactions without leaving the app. This gave rise to the Super Apps.

With decades under a single-child family policy, super apps are a godsend because of the additional responsibilities of a single child now required to take care of parents and grandparents. Reducing shopping steps from browsing to payment minimizes the time to take on life's menial tasks. User experience designed to reduce time on a platform is a vital part of any design application. Still, it is often taken to the extreme in China because Chinese consumers are traditionally more time-starved because of their family obligations than their western counterparts.

Super Apps also enabled Tencent and Alibaba to leverage more media money usually set aside for brand awareness building. By controlling more of the marketing sales funnel, from awareness to conversion, experience & loyalty, Super Apps can effectively handle a large portion of the brand's marketing budget, dramatically increasing their revenue share. These multiple, independent Super App platforms contribute to the need for a variety of specialty agencies servicing different requirements because it is becoming increasingly difficult for a single-agency partner to handle everything.

As a result, brands need more agencies, especially with e-commerce experience. The latest Agency Scope China report conducted in 2021 and 2022 shows that the average China brand has an average of 26 agency partnerships, with 81.7% of the respondents citing they prefer to work with an ecosystem of specialized agencies. Only 15.6% of surveyed brands stated they currently work with a traditional, single-agency model. Not surprisingly, 68.8% of the respondents cited e-commerce as their crucial scope of work because it is essential to sales conversion.

The Big Boys Lose Ground

The new advertising environment has provided both challenges and opportunities for multinational agencies, but usually, those that can build scale, such as WPP's Ogilvy or GroupM, Publicis or Dentsu, effectively win out. These shops have integrated their offerings and built large teams to deliver media throughout multiple channel offerings. Gone are the Mad Men-era days when small pockets of creative teams would dream up big idea advertising ideas. They have been replaced by a small creative factory full of fresh, inexperienced, low-paid graduates who crank dozens of social campaigns weekly.

While at MRM//McCann, my IKEA digital creative team included 18 designers and copywriters who developed over 2,200 different mini-campaigns and posts in a single year. If you didn't have scale like these agencies, you either specialized in a particular business facet or closed shop altogether. And because many of the international shops never bothered to invest in technology that would help them integrate into the Chinese digital ecosystem, many were pushed to close shop by nimble and innovative local shops who invested in applications that helped brands achieve maximum marketing performance. Companies such as LinkFlow, a local technology platform enabling market automation within the social media space, provided a more effective, locally relevant, and lower-priced solution than Oracle's Eloqua. Target Social, a SaaS-based KOL influencer measurement platform that uses AI technology to detect the brand of lipstick worn in a TikTok video, services hundreds of international consumer product companies. SaaS technology platforms for LinkFlow and Target Social became the foundational service that enabled them to enter the door of many consumer product companies, allowing them to expand their business into other services that are effectively tied to brand media spending. Foreign agencies without the technology tools can only form partnerships with these companies and offer strategic services above what these companies can provide. But being too far from real-time data, their strategic services are minimal, leaving those companies with the tools to take their place.

As local advertising, media, or technology platforms grew in prominence starting in 2017, so did the reputation that foreign agencies were losing touch with local consumers and that only local agencies truly understand the Chinese consumer mindset. Even foreign brands would turn to some specialized local shops, particularly for social media activation, because they felt they were getting deeper consumer insights and more actionable ideas. But the notion that a British, French, Japanese, or American agency network was out of touch with the local Chinese insight was utterly unfounded, simply because there were very few foreigners working in agencies in China during that time, and most of the agencies were operated and managed by local teams. It wasn't often insights that brands were looking for, but agencies that were agile and nimble enough to be able to change with the evolving Chinese market. Flexibility was a clear advantage the local shops had over their global counterparts.

Whether they are consultants or manufacturers, foreign companies in China often struggle with the degree of autonomy the headquarters gives them at home to manage. Given the differences and complexities of the China market, there's generally the belief that successful foreign entities here have, over time, given the China office more flexibility to grow their businesses as they see fit, provided, of course, they follow global ethical practices. But this evolution has taken many years to evolve, and companies, for the most part, would keep a tight rein on their China operations for decades, often managing the massive market out of their regional headquarters in Singapore, which was generally more of an excellent place to live for expatriate families. At the same time, China's rugged living standards and poor air quality seemed like a much inferior choice.

Following brands like Unilever, HP, and Nokia, advertising agencies made their regional hubs in Singapore for many years, hiring a team of expatriate experts in creative, strategy, and data who would fly Business Class around the region, hoping to satisfy regional client requests and help the markets identify new business opportunities.

But when China blocked Facebook in 2009 and Google departed in 2010, it triggered a new, China-only digital ecosystem that was later known as the "BAT"—Baidu (China's leading search engine), Alibaba, and Tencent, effectively decoupling China from the rest of the world. The rapid digital transformation in China, combined with the near eradication of paper cash in favor of payment apps, Alipay and WeChat, created a unique marketing ecosystem that further isolated the China market. It also signaled the end to market regionalization of brand assets such as television ads that were in the past created for multiple markets. For many global brands, China soon became its own independent entity. With Asia's largest market decoupled from the others, regional client business dramatically dwindled, signaling the end of the regional agency model.

Enter the Age of the Guochao

China was always a difficult market to predict for foreign brands because Chinese consumers are so ready to embrace change. Technology advancements are so intrinsically tied to the country's modernization that the masses more rapidly embrace new ways of connecting with friends, shopping, or entertainment compared to other markets. What took the global platform Facebook four years to reach 100 million users, Tencent's WeChat got in only a single year. China's latest obsession with short video platforms has also seen a massive transformation in how the Chinese engage in content. TikTok's China twin, Douyin, has gained enormous popularity, achieving 600 million daily active users as of 2021.

These rapid advancements and their subsequent take-up by Chinese consumers have also transformed the way people shop, both re-thinking the role of the traditional brick-and-mortar store and social media in how they impact e-commerce. China's online marketplace has rapidly evolved since Alibaba's Taobao launched over a decade ago. Chinese consumers in the cities have grown more sophisticated tastes. In contrast, the masses in lower-tier areas have become more value-driven, and the influence of word-of-mouth on social platforms, combined with the need for instant gratification, has led to the rise of casual shopping. Combining artificial intelligence curation and a labyrinth of influencer recommendations has forced brands to find new ways to reach and influence consumers. These platforms serve not just to satisfy the transactional needs of shoppers but help motivate consumers down new paths of product discovery.

Traditional retailers are no longer designed around product sales but product marketing experiences that combine entertainment with shopping. Some cosmetics retailers, including L'Oreal, have even started broadcasting livestream programming from traditional retail stores. Shop assistants no longer just attend to customers in the store but also engage with customers online. Nike's innovation center allows store customers to scan QR codes next to every product to discover shoe sizes and color options. The customer can then choose to purchase through the Nike app on their phone and have the convenience of the purchased shoes delivered directly to their home.

Thanks to China's massive production resources, product variations, and options can be quickly created and rolled out to the markets faster than anywhere else. Production supply chain advantages have given local brands the upper hand when launching new products, compared to their Western counterparts, who traditionally have a one-year development cycle for any new product, mainly due to global red tape. As a result, local brands can create new products quickly to satisfy the demands that evolve instantly through e-commerce algorithms or social media trends.

This behavior reflects a profound cultural difference between Western, Korean, or even Japanese business practices and their Chinese counterparts. While most international brands will meticulously research and test new product ideas for several months before launching to the public, Chinese consumer product companies will often blindly launch dozens of new products to the market, sometimes based upon gut feelings and flimsy data, hoping that one of them will be the unicorn. The reality is they know full well from the beginning that most of them will fail. This "moving forward through failure" method permeates almost every aspect of business, even in consumer technology. For the rare app successes to arise from Tencent, Alibaba, or Bytedance, there are hundreds of failures that never got anywhere. Shared bike apps Mobike and Ofo left mountains of defunct bikes on the streets as their funding dried up due to a lack of profits. China even had shared umbrella and basketball platforms for public courts.

With all these local products hitting the market, Chinese consumers began to see Chinese brands as becoming more innovative. The rise in new products launched by local players and the movement toward mobile commerce led to the pitch to the "*guochao*" (国潮) or "National trend" brands in 2020. *Guochao* brands claim to be particularly popular among China's GenZ born between 1995 and 2010. Unlike the older generations who idolized Western culture and brands, it is said that this generation grew up during China's meteoritic rise in the 2000s and thus had a stronger sense of national identity.

National pride also fueled the *guochao* movement during the Trump Administration's trade tariffs and the Xinjiang cotton crisis. Several global fashion brands, including Adidas and H&M, resolved not to buy cotton from any Xinjiang suppliers that may be using slave labor and were subsequently boycotted or banned. Some established brands, such as sports apparel brand Li Ning, even claimed they were a *guochao* brand and created a line of fashionable patriotic sportswear to jump on the bandwagon. Unfortunately, patriotism in any country is often a failed marketing strategy, and Chinese consumers generally go back to brands that deliver on their functional benefits or make them look cool.

Local brands are now a fact of the Chinese market reality and are growing in importance in the international agency portfolio of clients. Flooded with VC money, new *guochao* brands such as flavored soda water brand Genki Forrest are stealing share from the traditional leading players such as Coca-Cola. *Guochao* brands in categories with a closer pulse to local insights, such as food or fashion, tend to perform better than others. Still, some are simply inventing new and innovative ways to connect with consumers. China's leading EV automobile brand, NIO, prides itself on its owner loyalty program and even organizes club events for owners throughout its network.

One of my favorite *guochao* brands is Zhong Xue Gao, an innovative premium, high-priced luxury ice cream brand with a minimalist package design and tasty ice cream popsicles shaped to resemble clay roofing tiles that originated in the Zhou Dynasty. Zhong Xue Gao is unique as an ice cream brand in that it primarily sells online, so it invests heavily in visual cues that would be appealing as seen on a Chinese GenZ's mobile phone. Even, the plastic popsicle sticks are stunning, each containing a special message revealed after you devour your ice cream creation. Taking advantage of short China supply chains, the brand can quickly create new, innovative, limited edition flavors.

One of the more innovative *guochao* categories in recent years is the booming pet care industry, expected to become an $83 billion market by 2023. During the 11/11 "Singles' Day" e-commerce event in 2020, cat food became the top-selling category on Tmall Global, which serves Alibaba's cross-border eCommerce marketplace. With massive increases in pet ownership—a 300% increase since 2013, the entire pet care category has grown 600%, creating a wide range of *guochao* innovations that take on anthropomorphic characters of their owners, including daycare, beauty, food, and medical services. New online brands consistently spring up with so much growth potential, often following the most notable human beauty trends. One of the more innovative *guochao* pet care brands is Pidan, creating China's first "pet lifestyle" category on its own. While cat litter products account for 70% of its sales, its most unique products include specially designed cat food bowls and toys. Pidan has also recently launched a line of dog lifestyle products.

While China is the foundational market for these *guochao* brands, it is clear that many have global expansionary ambitions. Some *guochao* brands do not even exist in China and were designed for foreign audiences. Many of these brands are born and grown on Amazon, where China has become one of the platform's single biggest markets for global media spending, now totaling over $1 billion in media spending annually. By Amazon estimates, there are nearly 100,000 different companies engaging in international commerce from China, while only a very few companies reach the company's top-tier status. One brand, Anker, is mainly known for making computer and mobile peripherals such as phone chargers, power banks, headphones, and charging cables. In 2019, Anker generated around $954 million in revenue and is now the best-selling portable charger on Amazon. Despite being based in Shenzhen, China remains one of the company's future growth markets where the brand is largely unknown.

Is China Still Worth the Effort for Foreign Brands?

Is China worth all the effort global brands and their agencies, given its highly complicated infrastructure and consumer engagement model, loose regulatory controls, and lack of intellectual property protection? Google and Meta have been highly criticized for their monopolistic tendencies over their dominance of the global digital ecosystem. However, they are no match for companies like Alibaba and Tencent, who seemingly control almost every aspect of someone's daily life, from banking to entertainment, shopping, gaming, and social media. They control both the content and the rails from which it is distributed. Living in China without Alibaba's Alipay, Taobao, and Tencent's, WeChat is almost impossible. Both platforms have created mini-ecosystems that make all other mobile applications meaningless. More importantly, they control an unfathomable amount of consumer data that, with the possible exception of the Chinese government, is not shared with anyone.

Many famous brands have left China, and it is not just because of the strict internet censorship laws; it is often due to poor preparation and a lack of market understanding. Best Buy and The Home Depot's 2011 and 2012 exodus were probably the most famous examples. Still, many brands came with grandiose ambitions but have lost so much money that they have either left, like Old Navy in 2020, or dramatically reduced their China operations to a few outlets, such as Forever 21. Of course, it is the international brand failures that get much attention. However, there are far more local brand disasters in China because the market environment makes it extraordinarily difficult to make money. With over 300,000 brands competing to get noticed on e-commerce platforms such as Taobao and JD.com, there is an ongoing "race to the bottom" as brands drop their prices as high as 40% to get in the spotlight for a minute on a livestream program. With nine major shopping festivals held throughout the year, it is no wonder that Chinese consumers have become so addicted to discounts that buying at regular prices is only reserved for the top luxury brands.

The agencies are constantly asked to do more for less, with the brands being squeezed. In the past, advertising agencies would sign multi-year contracts with their client partners, building a strong, long-term strategic bond where a team of dedicated creatives and planners would work daily with their client counterparts to create advertising communications across the entire consumer journey. Retainer relationships are increasingly infrequent, and influential brand procurement departments now hold separate pitches for every project. Agencies have transformed into project pitch teams who have to manage a balancing act between their current clients and the new ones that they wish to acquire, increasing stress and overtime hours for the staff, who often see their pay raises controlled by regional agency leaders who are often more concerned with maintaining their jobs and their healthy 6-figure salaries.

The COVID-19 pandemic has isolated China due to its restrictive travel policies that wouldn't allow visitors into the country, but many senior agency leaders stopped coming to China long ago. Citing the protection of their senior leadership from unexpected kidnappings by Chinese officials in retaliation over Huawei's CFO Meng Wan Zhou's detainment in Canada, senior leadership from agency network IPG haven't set foot in China since 2018. IPG's largest agency, McCann Worldgroup, went as far as retrenching its regional leadership based in Singapore in 2021, further isolating China from the rest of the network.

Despite all of these challenges, there are many solid and compelling reasons for brands and agencies to be in China, and it's just not because of the size or consistent, steady growth of the consumer market. Being in China in the consumer marketing business in 2022 is like having a window into the future of how consumers will shop and interact with products. Brands can effectively gain experience and learning that they can apply elsewhere, mainly due to the digital transformation of the industry that is now considered further ahead than anywhere else and is expected to become a model for the rest of the world. Social commerce, for example, demonstrates the unique juxtaposition of social media and e-commerce in an enclosed digital ecosystem, which is unmatched anywhere else in the world. Social commerce now represents 16% of the total China e-commerce gross merchandise value while slowly taking off in the United States. China's rapid manufacturing and supply chain enable speed to delivery of new and innovative products pulled directly from shopping insights in real-time. In many aspects, China has taken the concept of Fast Fashion and applied it to every conceivable product category.

China's local brands have expanded globally, providing opportunities for international consultants and agencies who can help them grow worldwide. And it is not just Huawei, Lenovo, Xiaomi, and Tiktok that have become global powerhouses; there's also Nanjing-based, fast-fashion online retailer Shein.com, achieving $10 billion in revenue in 2020. Chinese auto brands NIO and BYD also have global ambitions. Global consultancies with a base in China will always fair better because they will simply be able to understand the unique cultural nuances of their Chinese clients, helping them grow brands that lead to higher margins and loyal consumers. Chinese brands now compete in almost every imaginable consumer category on Amazon but usually play in the discount brand space. Chinese headphone brands such as TaoTronics, Zihnic, and Tiksounds may have comparable products to Beats or Bose, but their products sell for up to four to six times cheaper. What is the difference? Simple, It is marketing, and there is nothing stopping them from catching up.

Mr. Bryce Whitwam *is a 25-year marketing communications veteran and one of Asia's pioneers in non-traditional advertising, including digital, data, social marketing, digital transformation, loyalty and CRM, retail, and brand activation. Fluent in Mandarin, Whitwam's China career has included senior positions at Ogilvy, Lowe, Nielsen, and most recently, CEO at MRM//McCann China. Whitwam has lived in Taiwan, Hong Kong, Thailand, and China. Based in Shanghai, he was the China CEO of WPP's Wunderman for almost 11 years, from 2008 to 2019, building a 400-person business from a small team of 28. Whitwam has an MBA from the Thunderbird School of Global Management & a Bachelor of Arts in Russian Studies & Political Science from the University of Minnesota.*

CHAPTER 6

China's Auto Industry: The Race to a Sustainable Future

Bill Russo

The automotive industry has historically been a major driver of innovation and economic development. We are currently facing a shift in the center of gravity for the industry, as new trends and technologies have commercialized at scale faster in China. Policymakers and industry leaders need to pay attention to this if we in the West intend to sustain leadership in mobility innovation, which has historically been a key driver of economic growth and job creation.

We are facing a secular and generational shift in the automotive and mobility sector. The rise of connected, electric, and autonomous cars requires that key stakeholders control critical technologies and supply chains. These stakeholders include national governments and industries that depend on this sector for their economic sustainability. Over the past decades, China has skillfully navigated its way to leadership in the

B. Russo (✉)
CEO of Automobility. Shanghai, China
e-mail: bill.russo@automobility.io

K. D. Gibbs (ed.), *Selling to China*,
https://doi.org/10.1007/978-981-99-1953-6_6

commercialization of innovative technology solutions linked to the future of mobility.

THE HISTORICAL IMPORTANCE OF MOBILITY INNOVATION

Throughout human history, mobility innovation has marked the advancement of civilization and has catalyzed economic development. Prior to the eighteenth century, people and goods movements were primarily limited to short distances. Longer distance movement would involve the use of animals (over land) or wind power (over water). Human activity and settlements were clustered in cities where longer distance transportation was via waterways, and canals were built to extend economic development inland (see Fig. 6.1).

The nineteenth century Industrial Revolution brought accelerated mobility technology innovation, as people harnessed the power of steam and carbon-based energy resources to power sea and rail transportation (see Fig. 6.2). The invention of the internal combustion engine (Carl Benz, 1885) eventually replaced the horse with an automated mobility device (the "automobile"), and 138 years after this innovation we still nostalgically rate the performance of these machines in "horsepower."

Fig. 6.1 Tow barge to Haarlem, Reinier Nooms, 1652–1654. Collection Rijksmuseum, Amsterdam

Fig. 6.2 Borsig's Maschinenbau-Anstalt zu Berlin in der Chausseestraße, Karl Eduard Biermann, 1803–1892

The twentieth century brought a stunning period of mobility innovation when transportation extended vertically into the air and outer space. Mass-produced automobiles, an abundant energy supply, and an expanding road and rail infrastructure also sharply accelerated economic development. Commercialization of air transportation vastly extended our range, and high-speed rail saw its initial deployment.

In the early twenty-first century, we stand at the threshold of a new era of mobility innovation, where advancements in energy density and performance are ushering in an era of electric propulsion. Advancements in information technology, artificial intelligence, and robotics will soon usher in an era of autonomous mobility, and these robotic movements on land and in the air will once again vastly expand economic activity.

CHINA AND THE AUTOMOTIVE INDUSTRY CENTER OF GRAVITY

China has contributed virtually all of the incremental demand growth in the twenty-first-century global automotive industry. In 2009, China surpassed the United States to become the world's largest market in new vehicle sales, and despite peaking at 28.9 million units in 2017, it remains by far the leading auto market in the world. Today, China accounts for more than 30% of global vehicle production.

As a result, the center of gravity of the global automotive industry has shifted eastward to markets with the highest global population and economic growth. Global automotive companies and their suppliers almost universally seek to deepen their participation in the China market as it represents the key battleground for dominance of the global auto industry. However, this battle will not be waged using the conventional automotive technologies which have prevailed for over a century.

In recent years, global carmakers are challenged to revisit and redefine their China strategy due to evolving geopolitics, trade tensions, shifting policies, and technological challenges facing the Automotive industry. In addition to this, the unique context of China's urban transportation challenge, the high penetration rate of mobile internet, combined with the rapid and aggressive introduction of alternative mobility and ownership concepts are transforming the underlying business model and thereby the economics of the industry in a manner that is not favorable to legacy carmakers. These developments are also serving to bifurcate the mature western markets (led by the US) from rapidly emerging markets (led by China).

Through a variety of methods, Chinese companies are accelerating the commercialization of connected, electric, and autonomous mobility technology and have thereby emerged as leaders in automotive and mobility innovation. As a result, China is now setting the pace for the transformation of the business model of an important global industry and moreover, is well positioned to dominate the global supply chain for the materials and technologies that power sustainable economic development.

The 4-Stage Journey from Industry Follower to Innovation Leader

The automotive industry has perennially been cited as a "pillar industry" in China's 5-year plan, meaning that it is prioritized as a key part of China's industrialization and modernization plans.

From the onset of China's reform and opening period, the Chinese government has required foreign carmakers to form joint ventures with local companies in order to produce and sell cars in China. The intent of this policy was to ensure that foreign companies did not simply come to China to extract profits from selling products, but rather to invest in building the critical infrastructure needed for an industry that China viewed as key to its forward economic development.

Foreign carmakers have done so in order to access the growth potential of the world's largest car market and avoid the penalty from import duty and transportation costs, which make imported cars less cost competitive. Decades later, it is now very clear that this policy has seeded the creation of a formidable supply chain, manufacturing, and technology commercialization advantage for China in the race to the future of mobility.

Stage 1: Global Automakers Enter China (1984–2000)

The advent of China's modern automotive industry traces back to 1984 with the formation of the initial Sino-foreign joint ventures Beijing Jeep Corporation (formed by American Motors Corporation and Beijing Automotive Industry Corporation) and Shanghai Volkswagen (formed by Volkswagen AG and Shanghai Automotive Industry Corporation).

Early on, auto industry sales were mainly light and heavy commercial vehicles. Passenger vehicle annual sales never exceeded 1 million units during this period. In this nascent stage, the goal of the Chinese government was to develop the automotive market with just a few players. During this period, foreign brands typically assembled vehicles from kits of parts shipped from overseas and localized manufacturing was minimal.

In 1994, the China Planning Commission (the predecessor of the National Development and Reform Commission) issued the Policy for the Automotive Industry ("1994 Auto Policy"). A key tenet was limiting foreign automakers to owning no more than 50% in any Sino-foreign joint venture (JV) as well as limiting foreign automakers to no more than 2 joint ventures for any single type of vehicle in China.

Later preference was given to internationally competitive manufacturers who committed to producing world-standard products from locally supplied parts. General Motors entered China in 1997 by partnering with Shanghai Automotive Industry Corporation (SAIC), bringing a strong commitment to localized production and sourcing in China.

As the twentieth century drew to a close, policymakers in China began to prioritize investments in establishing a leadership position in building a modern transportation sector. The target for this development was to prioritize investments into alternative propulsion technology, the area where global automakers had the most significant advantage, and where the incumbent solution, the internal combustion engine (ICE) had roots dating back over a century.

The initial target, starting in 1999, was compressed natural gas (CNG), liquid petroleum gas (LPG) and other combustion alternative fuel vehicles (CAFVs), in a program called the Clean Auto Auction. A second phase, coinciding with the Tenth Five Year Plan, introduced the goal to commercialize and industrialize electric vehicles. The National 863 Program targeted the Electric Vehicle Project and identified the Fuel Cell Vehicle (FCV), Electric Vehicle (EV), and Hybrid Electric Vehicle (HEV) as the priorities for the development of alternative propulsion technologies. Through this initiative, officials committed RMB 800 million from the State High Tech Development Plan, the government's leading advanced technology development program.

Even in its earliest stages of development, in a market that was fully dependent on overseas investment and government subsidies, there was clear intent on the part of China's policymakers to invest and build a leadership position in the twenty-first-century automotive industry.

Stage 2: WTO Accession, Foreign Investment, and the Exponential Rise of Auto Sales (2001–2009)

China's accession to the World Trade Organization in 2001 opened the floodgates of overseas investment in China's auto sector. In addition to GM, leading global automakers from the US, Europe, Japan, and Korea all established joint ventures to build and sell vehicles in China with local partners (see Fig. 6.3).

Global carmakers that followed the policy to set up joint ventures and localize manufacturing and supply chains have, in large part, been able to enjoy strong growth and profitability as the market exploded in size over this time period.

A rise in consumer buying power over this period saw passenger car sales rise from just under 1 million annual units in 2000 to over 10 million units in 2009. That same year, China surpassed the United States to become the largest automotive car market in the world (measured by new car sales), with overall sales of passenger and commercial vehicles of 13.6 million units.

In 2008, at the height of the Global Financial Crisis, the Chinese government unveiled a fiscal stimulus package of RMB 4 trillion (US$ 6 billion) to spur domestic demand and avert an economic slowdown (see

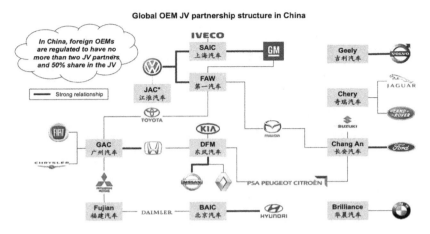

Fig. 6.3 Sino-foreign joint ventures in China

Fig. 6.4). This stimulus was focused on building economic momentum as well as solid transportation infrastructure. A modern nationwide high-speed rail network, as well as a modern airport and highway network, was created from these investments.

In 2009, the Chinese government continued to stimulate the market by announcing a tax cut on smaller cars and offering incentives on vehicle sales in rural areas. In the same year, the government issued an automotive industrial policy with eight development goals for 2009 to 2011. The goals were designed to ensure the steady growth of automobile production and sales in China and provide support for new energy vehicle research, aiming to leapfrog the developed markets with newer and more efficient propulsion technologies.

Through the use of the JV form of cooperation, the government policymakers hoped a domestic industry would emerge whereby the Chinese domestic companies would learn from their partners and eventually emerge as successful automotive companies. In theory, the domestic companies would learn from their foreign counterparts the skills needed to manage a complex business, establish manufacturing, and supply bases to produce vehicles and ultimately transfer critical technological development capacities in order to build their own locally branded products.

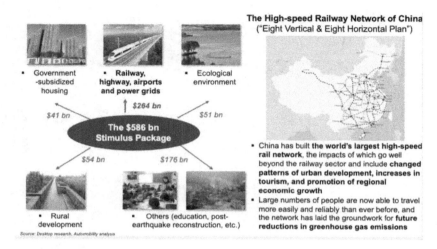

Fig. 6.4   Leveraging a crisis to build a modern transportation infrastructure

While China's automotive market indeed developed rapidly, the joint ventures with state-owned enterprises did not yield globally competitive carmakers. While an infrastructure to manufacture cars was established around JVs, no global-leading Chinese brands emerged as a direct result of the policy. The root causes for this can be traced to several factors, some of which include:

- JV structures (especially when there is equal shareholding) are difficult to manage resulting in strategic misalignment among the partners.
- Foreign partners are averse to sharing intellectual property (IP) around core automotive technologies with their Chinese partners.
- Lack of brand equity of local state-owned carmakers with Chinese consumers.

However, during this period we began to see the acceleration of cross-border investments in the Chinese automotive sector. MG Rover assets were acquired by Nanjing Automobile Group in 2005. In 2007, they began producing MG branded cars and the company was later merged with SAIC which retained control of MG and created its own local brand Roewe as an adaptation of the Rover brand name. In mid-2008, the privately-owned company Geely approached Ford about a possible takeover of Volvo Cars. It was named as the preferred buyer in October 2009 and completed the $1.8 billion transaction to acquire the company the following year. In September 2008, Warren Buffet took a HK$ 1.8 billion stake in privately held BYD, an up-and-coming battery company that was entering the automotive industry, through its Sino-American Energy Holdings investment arm.

In fact, today's leading Chinese domestic car brands such as Geely, BYD and Great Wall are privately-owned enterprises led by entrepreneurs, and their development was not dependent on foreign investment in joint ventures.

Stage 3: From Policy Driven to Market Driven (2010–2017)

During this stage, the automotive industry continued to rise rapidly from 18.1 million unit sales in 2010, to its all-time peak in 2017 at 28.9 million units. Passenger car sales rose in this same period from 13.5 to 24.7 million vehicles.

It is noteworthy that foreign investment in the form of new joint ventures slowed significantly over this period, with just a few late entrants (e.g., Jaguar Land Rover with Chery Automotive) entering the market from overseas. The industry was transitioning from its policy and investment-led beginning to a market-led development.

During this period, Chinese brands gained market share and increased their capability as traditional car makers. Chinese brands' share of the passenger car market nearly doubled from 2007 to 2017, accounting for 44% of the total sales of passenger vehicles, as they became the pacesetters for capturing opportunities in the fastest growing sport-utility vehicle segment, as well as first-time buyers in lower-tier regions of the country. However, the true disruption we are witnessing today did not emerge from traditional carmakers.

A significant development during this period was the advent of a new frontier of technology innovation: the emergence of pay-per-use mobility services. Traditional automotive Original Equipment Manufacturer (OEM) business models rely on selling products through an established business-to-consumer (B2C) channel, often through an intermediary sales partner (the car dealership) that is either owned or franchised to represent OEM brands in the marketplace.

China's internet giants (including Tencent, Alibaba, and Baidu) were actively investing in future mobility technologies (including connected, electric, and autonomous vehicles). These digital disruptors initially entered the mobility landscape by offering "pay-per-use" shared services. While pay-per-use mobility services had existed for some time in the form of centralized managed fleets (rental car companies, taxi and chauffeur services), digitally disruptive companies such as Uber, and Didi Chuxing (initially formed by merging separate mobility platforms from Alibaba and Tencent) gained rapid and widespread market acceptance in China.

These asset-light services-centric internet technology disruptors disintermediate the value chain of the automotive industry by democratizing access to personal mobility and breaking the requirement of asset ownership. This has profound implications for the long-term demand for individually owned vehicles and has brought an entirely new form of competitor into the market.

While shared mobility was not unique to China, its presence in China's densely populated urban centers made it far more disruptive to the industry in China than in the rest of the world for several reasons. For one, far more people ride than drive in China, and most of these riders do not have driver's licenses and have never owned cars. China's internet user base is over 1 billion people, virtually all of whom access the internet primarily through a smartphone. The explosive demand for pay-per-use mobility services has accelerated the entry of digital ecosystem players like Alibaba, Tencent, and Baidu into the automotive and mobility sector.

In the race to dominate the future of mobility, Chinese smart mobility and EV startups have quickly emerged and are rapidly expanding, backed by deep-pocketed investors who generate profits from China's booming digital economy.

China's new breed of Smart EV companies, including NIO, XPENG, and Li Auto, were established during this period. These and other "new game" players are creating digitally-enabled mobility solutions that shift the focus from selling product hardware (the "automobile") to providing a digitally-enabled business model centered on services.

Stage 4: Policy Shift and the Path to Electrification (2018-Date)

During a period of rising US-China trade tensions, China's President Xi Jinping announced at the Boao Forum in April of 2018 that measures would be taken to lower tariffs and relax restrictions within the auto sector. Shortly after President Xi's announcement, the National Development and Reform Commission (NDRC) revealed that foreign ownership limits on automakers would be phased out over a 5-year transition period. Viewed as a major initiative to further open China's economy, the proposal included the elimination of the 50% cap on foreign ownership in automotive manufacturing ventures. The cap would first be eliminated on foreign investment in New Energy Vehicles (NEVs), followed by the elimination of the cap for all types of ventures by 2023. In China's definition, NEVs are vehicles that derive their primary power from sources other than fossil fuels. These include battery-powered electric vehicles (EV), plug-in hybrid electric vehicles (PHEV), and fuel cell electric vehicles (FCEV).

China was essentially putting out the bait for the global EV producers to build their manufacturing and supply footprint for next-generation mobility technology in China, while at the same time conceding that a leading global EV brand would be needed to spark Chinese consumer interest in the technology.

Until this point, leading EV companies like Tesla had been reluctant to invest under China's JV requirements, viewing the 50% policy requirement as too high a price to pay for market access. Immediately after this announcement, Tesla seized the opportunity to build its footprint in China. In May 2018, Tesla announced a vehicle assembly manufacturing agreement with the Shanghai government to build its Gigafactory 3 in the Lingang free trade zone. Chinese authorities provided cheap land and low-interest loans, expecting in return that Tesla would groom local suppliers and spur the Chinese EV industry.

While China had for more than a decade promoted the investment in new energy vehicles and related infrastructure, there had been very limited consumer demand for these vehicles. Most electric vehicles were sold to fleets serving public transportation, government, taxi, or ride-hailing fleets and were heavily subsidized. Tesla's entry into the EV market in China sparked retail consumer interest in electric vehicles, which helped increase retail consumer demand across the entire sector (see Fig. 6.5 for the sales mix of leading players in 2019).

The mobility services segment played a critical role in the introduction of EVs, mainly driven by easier access to license plates for electric vehicles. As of June 2019, there were close to 1 million EVs registered with Didi, representing 35% of the total electric vehicle population across China.

The removal of foreign ownership joint venture restrictions was viewed as a signal of the Chinese government's increased confidence in their

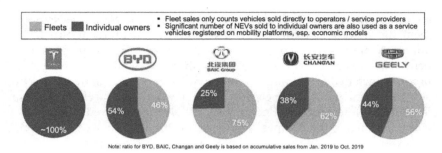

Fig. 6.5 Top EV OEM sales breakdown by customer segments in 2019 (%)

home-grown automakers and served as a stimulus to urge Chinese automakers to improve their products and strengthen their brands to compete with the global EV leader Tesla. It also gave foreign automakers the option to separate their China operations from their Chinese joint venture partners.

During this period, the Trump administration in 2019 implemented a series of tariff measures aimed at re-shoring industrial supply chains and making sourcing from China more costly. This began a period that has been referred to as the US-China "Trade War." While these measures were applied across a range of industries, the impact on the automotive industry was especially severe. For several decades, the global carmakers and suppliers were practicing what was commonly known as "low-cost country" (LCC) sourcing. As a market with massive scale and efficient logistics infrastructure, China had become the preferred place to source automotive components.

In effect, tariffs placed on content sourced from China resulted in higher cost of goods sold, eroding profit margins from automakers, and increased prices to American consumers. *If the trade war was a missile aimed at Beijing, the unintended consequence was that it landed squarely on Detroit.* Carmakers and suppliers were faced with the choice of passing on the added sourcing costs to the consumer, or otherwise taking a bite out of their profit margin.

Another unintended consequence was that the tariffs did very little to re-shore industrial supply chains. Rather, they accelerated investments into offshore locations from which Chinese suppliers could produce components for sale in the US, effectively accelerating the globalization of many Chinese companies.

In addition, the Committee on Foreign Investment in the United States (CFIUS), an inter-agency committee of the United States Government that reviews the national security implications of foreign investments in US companies, was placing additional scrutiny on Chinese capital investments in American technology.

While these measures may have been intended to place a check on the perceived threat from a rising China, they did not stop China's development and in fact may have redirected China's focus to acquiring technologies from other markets (for example fuel cell technology from East Asia and AI technology from Israel), while accelerating expansion of the supply chain and manufacturing footprint beyond China.

The unintended consequence of this was that technology firms in the US were cut off from important sources of capital. As a result, US technology firms operate in a bifurcated world that does not match the speed, experimental mindset, or scale of China's digital economy.

Furthermore, China's commitment to upgrading the industry was further reinforced in April 2020 when, in the immediate aftermath of the COVID-19 pandemic, the National Development and Reform Commission announced a fresh stimulus and investment in "new infrastructure" that would include infrastructure systems "based on information networks that provide data transition, smart upgrade and integrated innovation services."

President Xi Jinping announced "unprecedented spending on new infrastructure, including 5G networks and data centers, as well as accelerated expenditure on traditional projects including high-speed railway lines, will top China's response to the economic impact caused by the coronavirus outbreak." Just like in the aftermath of the global financial crisis, China was turning the crisis into an opportunity to accelerate the path to the future with "New Infrastructure" investments in critical areas (see Fig. 6.6).

China's Energy-Saving and New Energy Vehicle Technology Roadmap 2.0 was released on October 27, 2020, providing a roadmap for intelligent connected vehicles, new energy vehicles, and assisted and autonomous vehicle deployment over a 15-year period. Already far ahead of the rest of the world with nearly 47% of the EV charging capacity in the world in 2019, this fresh commitment would ensure that China remains far ahead of other markets in the deployment of public and private EV charging infrastructure.

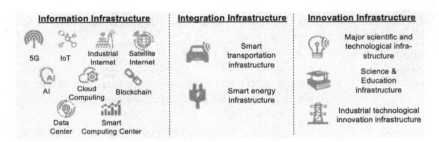

Fig. 6.6   Leveraging a crisis to build a modern smart technology infrastructure

Sales of New Energy Vehicles (including battery electric, plug-in hybrid, and fuel cell electric vehicles) have risen exponentially in recent years, rising rapidly to nearly 27% of overall vehicle sales in 2022 (see Fig. 6.7).

In a market where foreign brands have long dominated, Chinese local brands now have an early mover advantage in the electrification race, gaining a 11% market share increase since 2020 (see Fig. 6.8), and actually surpassed foreign brand sales in the 4th quarter of 2022. Foreign brands, which have historically dominated the auto sector in China, are struggling to get in the new game.

When looking at the list of the top global carmakers, it becomes clear that, with the exception of Tesla, all have considerably weaker market performance in 2022 (Fig. 6.9). These declines are directly related to a

Fig. 6.7   The rise of new energy vehicle sales in China

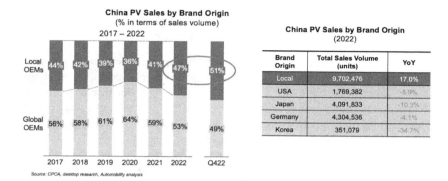

Fig. 6.8 Chinese passenger vehicle sales by brand origin

secular shift in market preference, which has not been favorable to foreign brands that have failed to properly position themselves for this market shift.

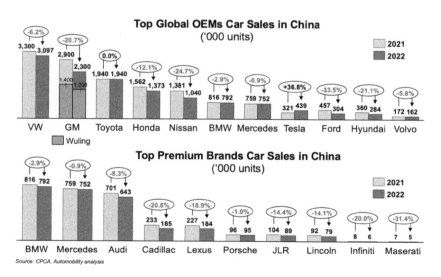

Fig. 6.9 Top global automakers in China, 2021 vs. 2022

Takeaways from China's 4-Stages of Auto Industry Development

While foreign observers see China as monolithic and centrally planned, its trajectory through these four automotive industry development stages was neither predictable nor the direct result of government planning. However, the government played an essential role in setting policy objectives, providing guidance, bootstrapping investments in infrastructure, and providing subsidies to the early movers.

This is a critical point that differentiates China: a massive ability to scale mobility solutions combined with a unique ability to leverage public and private partnerships (PPP) to drive the commercialization of high-tech innovation in line with policy objectives.

- China has achieved its position with strong central policy formulation and a vision for managing and investing in infrastructure and supply chains.
- China has a well-crafted central government policy with well-funded public infrastructure investments that have de-risked private sector investment. These are essential in emerging technology fields related to the Future of Mobility—especially for Artificial Intelligence, Intelligent Connectivity, and EV propulsion technology.
- China's emerging advantage has been accelerated by the rise of entrepreneurial private enterprises in the digital economy.
- China is a very efficient services demand aggregator due to its large and commercially aggressive Internet economy.

A Perfect Storm and the Decoupling of East and West

Since 2019, the automotive industry has experienced a perfect storm of both demand and supply shocks from the trade war and COVID-19 pandemic, which pose great challenges to the existing global supply chain (see Fig. 6.10). While global car sales have generally recovered, the lingering impact of the pandemic on the supply chain is still manifesting today, most recently in 2021 with the inability to secure a sufficient supply of semiconductor chips needed to build vehicles. This is directly linked to the post-COVID-19 spike in demand for chips used in the consumer electronics sector.

The sudden acceleration of demand for electric vehicles has placed additional pressure on the supply chain for the materials needed to produce batteries, resulting in an escalation of cost for electric vehicles. Further supply chain disruption has resulted from the Russian invasion of Ukraine in February 2022.

Coping with the combined impact of the trade war, the COVID-19 pandemic and multiple supply chain constraints have been a major distraction for global carmakers that were already contending with a hyper-competitive market, challenging JV structures, and the need to invest in next-generation connected, electric, and autonomous vehicle technology. Adding to this already challenging environment, the re-emergence of COVID-19 in the form of the Omicron variant resulted in an extended series of lockdowns across China, further roiling the already fragile supply chain. These challenges are accelerating the "decoupling" of Eastern and Western markets.

In order to anticipate how this industry may evolve going forward, as well as understand how these decoupled paths diverge, we will dive deeper into how China intends to leverage the "Internet of Mobility"

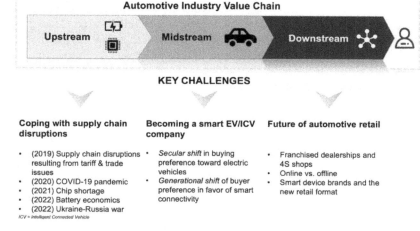

Fig. 6.10 Key challenges across the automotive industry value chain

to accelerate the commercialization of mobility-related technologies and related supply chains.

How Did Legacy Carmakers Get Stuck in the Slow Lane?

While the internal combustion engine was first used to power a car in 1885, Henry Ford's introduction of the moving assembly line in 1908 is what ultimately changed the world by democratizing personal ownership of automobiles. While we have witnessed great technological advances in mobility since this time, the business model and products of the automobile industry have only changed incrementally.

Unlike other everyday service-oriented devices such as phones and computers, cars, and trucks have somehow been impervious to a change in their external appearance. Phones have evolved from fixed-position devices providing basic telecommunication services to software-defined smart devices which provide access to services. The form factor of the phone has been altered from a wall-mounted wired device to a wireless internet-powered compute platform. Portable internet-powered smart devices now have the storage and computing power of water-cooled mainframe computers that filled entire rooms in the late twentieth century.

However, automobiles look pretty much the same as they did more than half a century ago. Despite having significant embedded electronics inside, automobiles are still designed for drivers with only a slightly modified form factor (see Fig. 6.11). In the future, we expect dramatic changes in the design of the smart mobility device.

While automotive form factors have only changed superficially, electronics and software sophistication have risen rapidly as more intelligent connectivity and smart device technologies are installed in vehicles. In the next few years, when electric and self-driving technologies become standard features of vehicles, automobiles will evolve into more personalized, user-centric form factors that are linked to a service-based mobility infrastructure—just like all the other smart devices we interact with every day.

New entrants—in particular, Chinese Internet technology companies who understand the market context—are serving mobility needs in a unique and innovative way. As a result, they are disrupting the core business of traditional automakers.

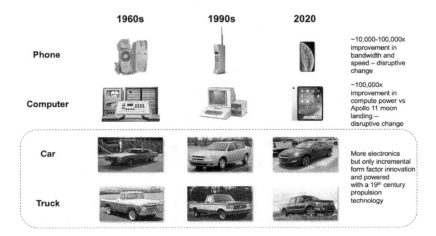

Fig. 6.11 Form factor innovation

COMPETING IN CHINA'S "INTERNET OF MOBILITY" GAME

China's emerging advantage is no longer a by-product of government policy and foreign investment. China has passed an inflection point of a secular and generational shift with a corresponding exponential rise of Smart EV technology. As previously noted, digital platform players are investing heavily to create devices that unlock new recurring revenue streams linked to mobility, energy, and other online and offline services.

Entrepreneurial private enterprises have emerged from the digital economy to invest in mobility innovation. As a result, the information and internet technology revolution that started in the late twentieth century is now acting as an accelerating force for mobility innovation. The creation and commercialization of the consumer-oriented internet have transformed devices we interact with daily into service-oriented and software-defined platforms.

The internet population in China reached nearly a billion users by the end of 2020, providing a huge market for services-oriented demand aggregation. As the market with the largest population of people, virtually all of which are served by mobile internet platforms, we are at the early stage of the mobility revolution sparked by the entrance of internet and communications technology (ICT) players in the mobility sector.

China's digital economy is setting the pace for an entirely new services-centric business model where "new game" commercial opportunities are created. This "new game" is highly embedded in the digital ecosystem and will change the car from a device monetized primarily when sold to a device monetized in multiple ways over its productive life cycle. New Game players often emerge from digital ecosystems, have experience monetizing other software-defined smart devices, and are highly efficient aggregators of services that are accessed through smart devices.

We live in an era where big data is used to provide personalized services that are often accessed through a smart device, powered by the mobile internet. These smart device technologies are now being incorporated into the devices that transport people and goods, which will revolutionize the business of how these devices are monetized. Transportation innovation has marked economic advancement throughout human history, and we are about to see this happen again as the internet economy enters the new game of smart mobility.

Mobility-related services provide access to daily life needs and conveniences, linking us between the places we live, work, and play. Multimodal traffic systems, parking infrastructure, charging stations, and public safety services are just some of the most visible elements. In China, such services are made available through public and private partnerships (PPP) at the local level, including health care, public safety, energy, and more.

China's auto sector has fully embraced the "Smart EV" or "Intelligent Connected Vehicle (ICV)" era. As a result, we are witnessing a rapid acceleration of the commercialization of new energy vehicle (NEV) propulsion technology and advanced driver assistance systems (ADAS), making mobility safer, more economical, and partially freeing the driver from the mundane task of actuating the vehicle movements.

This will lead to an autonomous mobility on demand (AMOD) era where people (robo-taxi) and goods (robo-delivery) movements are automated. Of course, driver-actuated mobility will co-exist with such devices, but the overall economic advantages of smart, autonomous vehicles will spark large-scale commercial deployment.

With its large and commercially aggressive digital economy, China is effectively transforming the traditional product-centric automotive industry business into a services-centric Internet of Mobility business model. When the vehicle is conceptualized as a smart device, it collects information on the users, the vehicle, and its surroundings. All the data generated from the vehicle and users can be uploaded to the cloud for

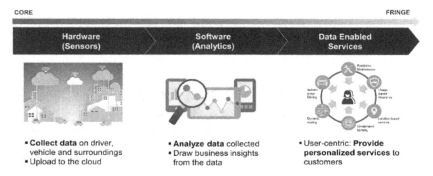

Fig. 6.12   Internet of mobility data monetization

analytics to better provide data-enabled services to users in vehicles (see Fig. 6.12).

The unique combination of urban mobility, high penetration of mobile internet, along with the rapid and aggressive introduction of shared mobility solutions provide China with advantages in the ability to scale mobility innovation. In addition, public–private partnerships (PPP) are essential to spark innovation and to de-risk investments in new technology sectors (such as Intelligent Connected Vehicles,/Electric Vehicles/Autonomous Vehicles), and China has leveraged investments in infrastructure to accelerate the commercialization of new technology.

Competing in the New "Internet of Mobility" Game Takeaways

- The shocks of the trade war and pandemic have bifurcated the Eastern and Western markets, with China pulling ahead in the electrification race.
- Automakers are now reallocating capital plans and investing in electric mobility platforms & technology.
- Investors have assigned a huge market valuation to Tesla and a new class of Smart EV OEMs (NIO, XPENG, Li Auto) are emerging with "digital DNA."
- Smart device makers (Xiaomi, Huawei, Apple) are new potential entrants to the Smart EV game, who see the car as a platform for digital services and high-frequency user engagement.

- A new class of Smart EV and Smart Device players is transforming the traditional automotive business model as vehicles become smart devices.

THE GLOBAL RACE TO SUSTAINABLE MOBILITY

The race to sustainability is not just about green energy, but is more broadly a high-tech race for control of the resources that power sustainable economic development.

With global economies recovering from the COVID-19 pandemic, energy demand is surging. As renewable energy has not yet scaled to meet the growing demand for energy, fossil fuels have experienced a rebound. As the largest consumer of energy, and the main source of greenhouse gas emissions, a pivot to sustainable energy resources for powering transportation has become a national priority for China.

As a pragmatic short-term measure to counter recurring energy shortages across the country caused by the surging post-COVID-19 energy demand, China is planning to build 43 new coal-fired power plants in the upcoming years. This will effectively cancel out any positive impacts on emissions coming from the adoption of electric propulsion.

China has also announced its goal to become carbon–neutral by 2060. Part of the plan is a full transition to New Energy Vehicles (NEV) by 2035. This transition, however, will only lead to a reduction in greenhouse gas emissions (GHG) if China can successfully reduce its dependency on carbon electricity generation and introduces policies to incentivize NEV owners to use electricity generated from GHG-friendly sources.

China is also gradually liberalizing the power sector by lifting price caps, compelling some manufacturers to cut production and increase energy efficiency. Although the automotive industry is high on the list of protected sectors with regard to energy shortages, some isolated instances of energy-related disruptions have been reported along the automotive value chain in 2021.

The technology innovations needed to power the future of mobility will require the control of critical technologies and supply chains. While China has invested heavily in building a modern smart transportation infrastructure, it has also prioritized gaining an edge on the upstream battery and materials supply chain. With rising demand for electric vehicles, the global electric car battery market is now a $27 billion per year business.

The top 10 EV battery manufacturers are all headquartered in Asia, concentrated in China, Japan, and South Korea (see Fig. 6.13). Achieving energy security for accessing the resources required to power the domestic economy is a key objective in the push for sustainability. A stable and secure supply chain of materials is essential to ensure sustainable economic development.

While China has achieved an early mover advantage in the race to electrification and the associated battery supply chain, there are lingering weaknesses. China is an inefficient supply chain aggregator owing to its tendency to fragment its own regional markets while relying on (primarily) state-owned manufacturing enterprises to deploy policy and allocate capital at the local level.

While US firms have moved only incrementally on the commercialization of new mobility technology, the US possesses a world-class engineering and computer science talent pool, is backed by efficient

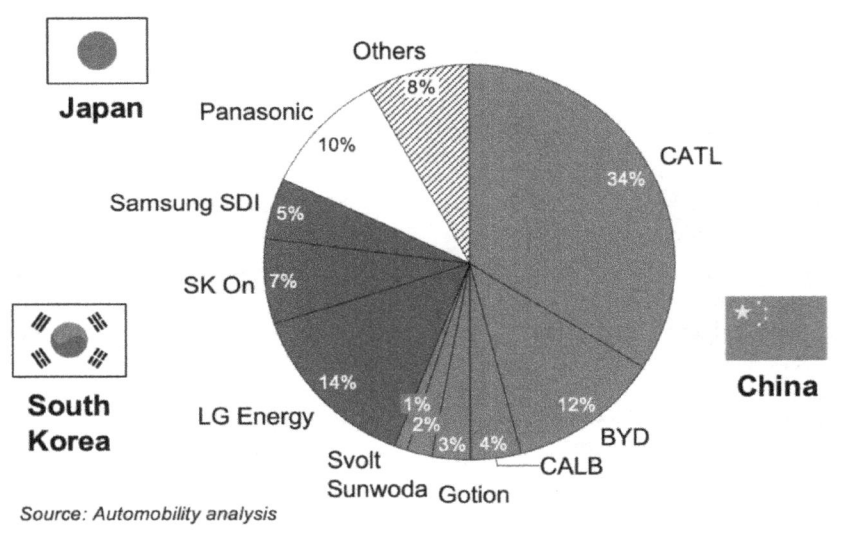

Source: Automobility analysis

Fig. 6.13 The global market share of world's leading EV battery pack players in 2022

capital markets that reward innovation, and is guided by a historically innovative and entrepreneurial culture. However, this does not overcome the inertia of an industrial sector that is risk averse and rooted in a century-old business model and lacks a clear national vision on the critical role of mobility in driving high-tech innovation.

Key Automotive Industry Questions for 2022 and Beyond

- Have Chinese brands turned the tables and gained a sustainable advantage over foreign brands in the EV race? Can global OEMs catch up?
- Can Chinese brands hold their gains as multinational carmakers enter the EV game in China?
- Should multinationals restructure their businesses in China in the EV era, now that they can own more shares? Does this even make sense as the market preference shifts to digital and user-centric services?
- Can Chinese carmakers translate their EV relevance and value propositions to become globally successful brands in other markets, especially in Europe and the US?
- Weighing Risks and Opportunities: Stay or Go?

The Industry View

Bifurcation of the East and West is not an ideal outcome for the automotive industry. This will effectively slow the rate of innovation, create two sets of incompatible industry standards, result in higher barriers to trade, reduce cross-border investments, and lower profitability due to dis-economies of scale.

A full decoupling would ultimately lead to a loss of Chinese market access for Western companies and potentially introduce more global supply chain complexity. Companies will attempt to re-shore supply chains to protect capacities, driving up costs and limiting access to global innovation and talent.

Viewed through the automotive industry's lens, China has been a source of profitable growth for global automakers with a commitment and conviction to invest and localize products together with domestic manufacturing partners. Automotive component suppliers, without policy restrictions requiring local partnerships, have also leveraged China to improve their global scale and cost competitiveness.

Of course, intellectual property leakage to Chinese copycats has always been among the chief concerns for the industry, along with the perceived lack of fairness of policies that are perceived to "force technology transfer" to China. However, it is clear that leading global carmakers who played the game wisely in China have been rewarded for doing so.

However, the game is changing in a manner where traditional carmakers and suppliers may not enjoy similar opportunities going forward. The shocks of the trade war and pandemic combined with the pivot to electrification and the emergence of new competition from Chinese technology players have raised legitimate questions as to whether risks now outweigh rewards. Control of supply chains for energy (batteries and raw materials), rare earth elements, and semiconductor chips, as well as data and information security risks make the case for investing in China even more complicated.

Next-generation vehicles will be smart, electric, and autonomous. Expanding demand for advanced electronics and IoT-ready features is redefining global automotive supply chains. For carmakers and suppliers, controlling critical technologies and supply chains such as semiconductors, lithium-ion batteries, alternative powertrains, and autonomous driving technology is crucial to their future success.

To remain relevant, industry players must invest to compete in a modernizing industry that is fast replacing its legacy business model and products—and they must decide whether they can compete in a Chinese market where requisite capability sets are changing rapidly and new capabilities must be acquired inorganically.

The historical pattern of mobility innovation driving economic advancement is clearly understood, and China is seizing this as a window of opportunity to build a sustainable domestic economic advantage. This is entirely analogous to how the US gained its advantage in the twentieth-century internal combustion era.

Carmakers and suppliers are challenged to invest in and/or build strategic alliances and ecosystem partnerships with new players including raw materials suppliers, battery makers, chipmakers, and internet companies that leverage their platforms to participate in the Internet of Mobility era of the twenty-first century, where China has clearly established an early mover advantage.

Without China, global carmakers and mobility tech companies will be hard-pressed to match the pace and scale of development and deployment of innovative mobility products and services and related infrastructure. With the proper approach, engagement in the Chinese mobility market presents an opportunity to explore new technology frontiers.

Collaborative innovation with Chinese partners can help build system-wide benefits for scaling the commercialization of technology and thereby improving the competitiveness and profitability of products sold internationally. This was a clear motivating force behind Tesla's recent entry into the China auto market.

THE MARKET VIEW

By any measure, China is the largest automotive (unit sales) and mobility market (vehicle miles traveled) in the world. Over one-third of cars sold in the world are sold in China, with over half of them carrying a foreign brand in 2022. China's addressable consumer market, innovative internet giants, as well as digital services economy are unrivaled in size anywhere on the planet. Chinese consumption is expected to double in the next decade with a focus on services over goods.

Participation in the China market is especially important when considering that the digital revolution extends beyond hardware sales. When a car becomes an Internet of Mobility device, its users become consumers of services linked to the mobility platform. Chinese consumers are more open to experimentation with new mobility solutions, especially deployed in China's dense urban environments. These make China a fertile environment to drive innovation and scale these solutions globally.

STAY OR GO TAKEAWAYS

- Trade policy and industry regulations should prioritize ensuring that markets remain open, collaborations are encouraged, and competition is on a level playing field in the twenty-first century mobility market.
- Slowing the pace of innovation to protect traditional markets and industry players will not yield a sustainable competitive advantage in a high-tech world.
- Efforts to contain China have accelerated the globalization of Chinese companies, as they seek to avoid tariffs.

- China will rebuild partnerships with other regional players if the US and other mature market players disengage.
- Collaboration and engagement is the best option, even if it gets more complicated.

Building a Sustainable Future

Throughout history, mobility innovation has been a catalyst for economic development. The competitiveness of nations is directly linked to having the capabilities to build and deploy innovative mobility solutions.

China has skillfully navigated its way to a leadership position by encouraging investment in areas where domestic capabilities were initially lacking. China no longer requires foreign capital to grow its automotive and transportation sector, and Chinese carmakers are developing rapidly and gaining market share without the aid of joint ventures.

Competing in the race to a sustainable future requires strong central policy formulation and a vision for investing in infrastructure and supply chains, especially for AI, Intelligent Connectivity, and EV propulsion technology. This serves to de-risk investments from the private sector which are essential in emerging technology fields related to the Future of Mobility.

China pursues technology partnerships from global innovation sources in North America, Europe, and Israel. Global technology firms need access to markets that can scale up innovative technology. As the world's most progressive market with a vibrant digital economy, China is the ideal place to deploy and scale new technology. Leveraging this, industry players should leverage their global presence and technology advantages to engage Chinese innovation ecosystems via M&A, strategic partnership, joint R&D, and joint ventures.

Tactics such as a trade war and/or forced technology transfer through joint ventures weaken the sector by introducing barriers to collaboration and investment. When confronted with Chinese disruptors, a better option would be to embrace "co-opetition," rather than resorting to anti-competitive trade protections. The world will be a better place if the race to the future is won by outpacing, not weakening, the competition.

Mr. Bill Russo *is the Founder and CEO of Automobility Limited and the former regional head of Chrysler in North East Asia. His 40 years of experience includes 15 years with Chrysler and 18 years working in China and Asia. He also worked for over a decade in the electronics and information technology industries, with IBM Corporation and Harman International. He has been an advisor and consultant for numerous multinational and Chinese firms in the formulation and implementation of their global market and product strategies. Bill Russo is currently serving as the Chair of the Automotive Committee at the American Chamber of Commerce in Shanghai. Mr. Russo has a Bachelor of Science in Chemical Engineering from Columbia University in New York and a Master of Science in Manufacturing Systems Engineering from Lehigh University in Bethlehem, Pennsylvania. He is a highly sought-after commentator and opinion leader on the development of the China market and the automotive industry.*

CHAPTER 7

Sports Marketing in China: Ball and the Wall

Mark Fischer

My career of more than three decades in greater China has been both rewarding and enjoyable. I've had the good fortune to lead the ground-up expansion of both NBA and UFC in Asia, and since then to build several other successful sports enterprises in the region. I learned to value Chinese culture and especially the Chinese people. I married one, made close friends with many, and worked alongside or competed with hundreds more—on and off the court. This adventure has of course also brought its fair share of unique challenges.

China has a complicated relationship with sports, as I learned when speaking with Mr. Yan Qiang, one of China's leading sports journalists and former chief editor of *Titan Sports* (体坛周报), in 2009. "From a cultural perspective, China is an anti-sports nation," he remarked to my surprise. "Sports go against some of our Confucian philosophy and traditions, which emphasize education and social harmony. And in modern China there is so much pressure to get ahead, or at least keep up, academically and financially. Most parents in China want their kids to spend all

M. Fischer (✉)
CEO of Fischer Sports & Entertainment. Boston, MA, USA
e-mail: mark@fischersea.com

© The Author(s), under exclusive license to Springer Nature
Singapore Pte Ltd. 2023
K. D. Gibbs (ed.), *Selling to China*,
https://doi.org/10.1007/978-981-99-1953-6_7

their spare time studying, so that they can score high on the *gāokǎo*.[1] Not waste their time on sports! So it has been a huge challenge for sports to take root in China."

Yan's observation left me stunned. Over the years I've come to learn that he was right in many ways, but not entirely. Somehow, the NBA managed to carve out a successful business. How was this possible in an "anti-sports nation?" How could I, as an athlete and sports marketing professional, carve out a career in this environment, and what lessons can I pass along about how things work in China, and about the culture?

BALLIN' FOR THE BANK: AN EARLY LESSON

Years before starting work for the NBA, I received a firsthand introduction to the Chinese sports mentality, and how different it was from that of westerners and especially Americans. It was also an early lesson of how the concept of "face," along with the related social hierarchies involved, reigns supreme in Chinese society.

I was just twenty-four years old and fresh off the plane in Taipei, my first time ever in Asia. While still a novice in all things Chinese, I was already a relative expert at basketball, as a six-foot-three gym rat with enough game to excel in high school and city-league basketball, but not enough natural talent to play Division I college. Soon after my Taipei landing, however, my play on the pickup courts of Taiwan University impressed a friendly local participant enough for him to introduce me to the head coach of a team in the island's top league. Coach Tian eventually offered me a tryout and a coveted spot on the Bank of Taiwan squad.

The league was semi-professional, meaning each of its players was an employee of the bank in some other capacity. Usually, as in the case of Bank of Taiwan, that meant working for the Marketing Department. In fact, none of the team's hoopers ever actually went to the company offices, and their "marketing" work consisted of wearing uniforms displaying the bank's name. The salary was less than $1000 a month, so I wasn't about to quit my day job as the Taiwan bureau chief for an electronics trade journal. But those were just details in the bigger scheme. I jumped at the chance to get paid to play the sport I loved and fulfill my childhood dream of becoming a "pro ballplayer."

---

[1] The *gāokǎo* (高考) is the national school entrance exam that is so critical in China to a student's future.

Once I got going with the team practices, however, a few things struck me as unusual, at least relative to everything I'd known to that point about how team sports work. First, around 90% of the two-hour daily practice regimen was spent on fundamental drills, running, and walking through plays. At the end, just a few minutes of each session were left for scrimmaging full-court 5-on-5. This seemed crazy to me. One would think that we would spend more time playing the actual sport, and gelling as a team on the court, not to mention having a bit of competitive enjoyment of the game.

All that said, after two months of this staid practice regimen, it was finally time to get on with what I'd signed up to do: play the games. The Chung Cheng Cup was in those days the island's premier basketball competition. All of the dozen or so participating teams were title-sponsored by big Taiwan companies such as our bank, and the likes of Yue Loong Auto, and Lucky Cement. The competition was held in Taipei's largest indoor arena, the Chinese Sports and Culture Stadium located on Nanjing East Road in the city's center, known locally as the *fànwǎn* (饭碗), or "rice bowl" for its white color and shape.[2]

The arena's 10,000 seats were filled to the rafters as I stepped onto the court to warm up for our first game. Basketball was already Taiwan's most popular sport (despite the island being better known internationally for its baseball prowess), and in those days of martial law live entertainment options were limited. So even though the actual level of play was probably not much higher than collegiate Division II or III in the United States, it was the only game in town and a hot ticket.

By the time of the tournament, I had worked my way up within the team from a novelty walk-on, as one of only three foreign-born players in the league, to one of the first two rotation players off the bench. Midway through the first 20-minute half, the coach called my number. I felt nervous playing in front of such a large crowd but ready to compete and give it my all. I hit my first few shots and hustled for several rebounds and steals, turning the crowd reaction from jeers to cheers, and ended the half with 12 points. More importantly, our team went from being down by 10 to ahead by 5, a 15-point swing during my brief appearance.

I was excited to play the second half, thinking for sure I'd get called in even earlier than the first. Instead, I got no minutes at all. Our team lost

[2] The venue burned down to the ground, rumored by arson for insurance reasons, several years later.

the lead and eventually the game by double figures. Upset at this turn of events, I went straight to Coach Tian and asked him why I didn't play the second half despite an obviously successful first run. He answered flatly, "you need time to understand basketball in Taiwan," and walked away.

It was only later, after prodding a couple of my local teammates that I learned what the coach really meant: I needed to learn more about Chinese culture, specifically the concepts of hierarchy and face. As it turned out, and completely unknown to me at the time, my success in the first half caused two problems. First, I had gone in—as an unknown rookie with no established status in the league hierarchy—replacing our best player, a Taiwan team member several years older. Second, by excelling in his absence, I had caused both the player, and in some way the coach by extension, to lose face. Even with that explained to me, I remained incredulous that face was more important than winning in a competitive basketball game.

I went on to play in similarly odd spurts for the rest of the tournament, and the team finished in the middle of the pack, apparently just as expected. I decided that this would be the beginning and the end of my career playing professional basketball, but I took away valuable lessons. First, face permeates everything in Chinese society, on and off the court. Second, Chinese training, including education at all levels, is based more on repetition and improvement of a pre-set routine, and less on creativity and the ability to problem-solve spontaneously. I would come to appreciate both of these important points as I embarked on my career in greater China.

Taiwan and mainland China have common cultural roots. They have the same Confucian system of values and ways of dealing with others in direct familial and societal environments, and a generally hierarchical social system promoted by a top-down education methodology. Yet Taiwan is arguably more Chinese than the mainland, with longstanding traditions that escaped getting diluted by communism or the Cultural Revolution, as they were in the People's Republic in the second half of the twentieth century. The Taiwanese people are generally well-educated and hard-working, but also fun-loving, warm, and affable. Taipei was a wonderfully hospitable landing point for my first years in Asia, and a great place to start unpeeling the thick onion of Chinese culture. Taiwan is also where I launched my career with the NBA in 1997. Taiwan by then was already a strong market for basketball, with Michael Jordan/Chicago Bulls jerseys—both authentic and counterfeit versions—a popular piece of apparel amongst the island's youth. Ultimately, the NBA's experience in Taiwan served as an excellent precursor, or "incubator," for entering the mainland China market.

The Go-Go Years: Yao and NBA China

In June of 2002, a seven-foot-six-inch center from the People's Republic of China became the NBA's number one draft pick. China had entered the World Trade Organization the year before, and the league was excited about the additional fan following and licensing revenue that a Chinese player could generate from the world's largest population.

Long before Yao Ming joined the NBA, China had already developed an affinity for basketball. Christian missionaries introduced the sport to China 100 years earlier, soon after the game's invention, and basketball was one of the few sports Mao continued to allow during the Cultural Revolution. NBA games had been aired on delay by then sole national TV sportscaster CCTV-5 since 1987, and Yao grew up admiring the post moves of mid-1990s NBA MVP Hakeem Olajuwon. Michael Jordan was already as much of an icon in China as he was in the United States.

Even so, getting the NBA offices set up and hiring a full-time staff on the ground in China was no layup.

Yao Ming was not the first player from China to play in the NBA. The seven-foot center Wang Zhizhi joined the Dallas Mavericks in 1999, but he never fulfilled playing expectations there, or during his short-lived stints with the Miami Heat and Los Angeles Clippers. He grew up within the Chinese sports system, with all its emphasis on repetitive drills and issues of face. He spoke almost no English and was too shy both on and off the court for the aggressive style of American basketball.

Making matters worse, Wang angered Chinese officials for failing to follow exit protocols on his way out of China, and then refusing to return to play on China's military and national teams when called. Chinese people love a winner, but sadly Wang had failed to check that box. Instead he became almost a pariah, which did nothing to fulfill the NBA's hopes for generating business in China.

The league's early efforts to establish a business had also been challenging. NBA Commissioner David Stern traveled to Beijing in 1989 to meet with the national broadcaster, CCTV. The legendary sports executive waited two hours in the lobby before senior officials finally came out to meet him.[3] Stern left with a modest win, an agreement to send over tapes of NBA games that CCTV-5 would air on a weekly basis. The league then began setting up and staffing offices in Hong Kong, Taipei, and Tokyo, but still generated almost no revenue from China. We had a few merchandise and media licensing deals, but the China market had yet to prove it loved the NBA enough to spend real money on it.

Chinese media and brands were still evolving from a state-run economy where consumer choice was limited, which made marketing all but unnecessary. These domestic entities had barely begun to promote their own brands with traditional advertising, let alone expand their marketing mix to include sports and entertainment sponsorship. In fact, few Chinese brands even understood the basic concepts and potential value of sports marketing, so it took considerable time and effort to educate them before they would actually pay for endorsements or other forms of brand association.

Meanwhile, NBA lawyers were wary of setting up a company and hiring staff in what was an uncertain and arbitrary regulatory environment. Despite the large market potential, for every China success story there were also stories about international companies getting burned in one way or another, whether a joint venture falling apart, financial challenges, or misuse of intellectual property.

So while I knew our business would take off as long as we invested enough resources toward the effort, the front office in New York needed convincing. Fortunately, Yao Ming was just the guy to get that done.

After taking a month or two to acclimate to the faster pace of the NBA game, by mid-season Yao became a strong contributor to the Houston Rockets. He could clog the middle on defense with his massive frame, and with his finesse became a strong low-post option on offense. But it was his game in January 2003 against the Lakers and their (future) Hall of Fame center Shaquille O'Neal that served as Yao's NBA coming-out party. Shaq versus Yao, the clash of two giants (both famous enough to go by one name) that some described as symbolic of the growing

---

[3] The story was later further embellished to note that the commissioner had to wait outside in the cold.

competition between their home countries. Yao started the contest with a surprising flourish, blocking two of Shaq's inside attempts and scoring with a pair of deft short shots on the other end.

The Rockets ultimately beat the first-place Lakers in overtime, but just as importantly, Yao proved himself a worthy competitor against the game's top big man. Soon thereafter, Yao topped Shaq in the NBA's worldwide All-Star balloting to start in the 2003 NBA All-Star Game. Shaq remarked that with fans able to vote online for the first time, the vote must have been skewed by the millions of Chinese voting for Yao.

Those of us working passionately on growing the NBA's brand in China took pride in Yao's selection, despite the balloting controversy. We had concluded our first major deal to license the Chinese version of NBA.com (to then leading Chinese internet company Sohu.com) earlier that season and created a nationwide promotion for fans in China to vote for the All-Star starters online via the new Chinese website. As NBA commissioner David Stern dryly noted when introducing Yao at a business function soon thereafter, "He's the leading vote-getter in the history of any election in China."

With Yao Ming thus established as an NBA star, the "Year of Yao" in full swing, and fans across China getting pumped up about basketball, our media team rapidly expanded the number of games televised in China. Most stations demanded Yao's Rockets games, but accepted the rest of the league's teams as part of the deal. We had to move quickly to convert the new exposure and fan momentum into revenue from China. We needed deals to justify the additional resources required to develop the large and fast-growing market.

In addition to the immaturity of sports marketing as a business, the Chinese government's control of media presented another major obstacle. Unlike the global market where media rights (meaning television content) provided the majority of revenue for major sports properties like the NBA, in China the government put an effective cap on media rights fees. Even the NBA, with a huge fan base in China, had limited negotiating leverage over CCTV-5.

To get around the national-level broadcast monopoly, our media team found a way to work with regional and provincial-level sports channels. These smaller channels could not pay large fees but they were eager for content. This gave us the exposure we needed to increase our negotiating leverage with CCTV-5. We eventually achieved satisfactory terms with the national broadcaster, securing four minutes per game of barter advertising time that we could then sell directly to our own brand partners for significant revenue.

Deals with Chinese companies relied on building trusted relationships at both leadership and mid-level management levels, usually requiring an elaborate series of conversations, often in unorthodox settings. Our first big deal—with the Hua Bin Group, owner of the China franchise for Red Bull energy drinks—was closed over drinks in my Beijing hotel suite after my colleague and their general manager paid me a surprise visit late one evening, and I answered the door in my bathrobe.

Setting up that handshake took months of regular visits to Hua Bin's headquarters in Beijing. We carefully cultivated a relationship with Yan Bin, the gregarious Thai-Chinese group chairman, who pontificated and regaled us for hours over elaborate meals and fine wines at his mansion, styled after the Palace of Versailles.

With that said, the efforts spent building relationships with Hua Bin Group was nearly matched by those spent working out approvals and contract terms with NBA headquarters. The league was concerned about how our partnership with a drinks company in China could adversely affect our longtime global relationships with Coca-Cola and Gatorade. We ended up going through a similarly complex process for most of our China deals, given the unique requirements and significance of the market. Any executive working for a multinational company in China needs to be prepared for considerable educating and negotiating, both internally and externally.

Eventually, this first big deal was sealed in time for the start of the 2003–2004 season, with fees that doubled NBA China's revenues from the previous year. Red Bull China produced billions of little gold cans adorned with eight designs of multiple NBA players and teams.

Chinese brands began taking notice, not only of Yao's phenomenal impact but also of the NBA's growing popularity among the general public. The passionate following among younger and upwardly mobile Chinese consumers was palpable. After years of networking, prospecting, and pitching to anyone who would listen, we started getting incoming calls from potential partnership clients. New York finally approved formal branch offices in Beijing and Shanghai, and additional marketing, events, and sales staff dedicated to building NBA China.

In February of 2004, we announced the first-ever NBA China Games, matching Yao's Houston Rockets against the championship-contending

Sacramento Kings. This event would bring two full NBA teams, not just a few players, to compete officially in China for the first time in history. Fans in China were ecstatic. All 30,000 tickets to the two games sold out immediately. The games, although meaningless to the regular season standings, captured a huge television audience across China. NBA China was on the map, and about to go on a roll.

We conducted national surveys with extrapolations indicating that the NBA had by then garnered 300 million fans in China. The 300 million figure was later adapted by the CBA and others to represent the number of basketball players in the country, but no matter. In the three-year period from the 2004 China Games through the Fall of 2007, we did so many new deals in China that we had a hard time announcing all of them. We could only fit so many press conferences into the calendar (Again for face, Chinese companies usually require big announcement events as part of any major new initiative).

Staffing up the China offices to keep up with the market demand was particularly challenging in those heady days. The sports marketing industry was still very new and niche, as was the corresponding talent pool. We had to utilize a mix of nationalities, bringing in experienced hands who generally were from overseas, while attracting and training up as many local Chinese staff as we could. A combination of PRC local, overseas Chinese (from Hong Kong, Malaysia, Taiwan), and western talent (North America, Europe, Australia) worked well for us then. This sort of mix may prove harder for international companies to achieve today, however, given China's heightened restrictions on travel and visas. On the other hand, there is a much larger pool of PRC nationals working in the sports business today.

The rapid growth of NBA China during those years also attracted interest from the investment community. Goldman Sachs approached the league with the idea of restructuring NBA China into a separate entity that would be able to take on third-party investors. The new structure made sense from a number of angles. First, the sale of shares in the new entity would put a real valuation on the entire league, with China as a proxy for NBA globally. This enabled each of the league's 30 owners, who collectively own NBA properties and all its subsidiaries, to participate in the upside in value from an NBA entity other than their own team. Secondly, options in the new China entity could provide equity incentives for management. Finally, the thinking went, strategic Chinese investors in the new entity would move the NBA into, or at least closer to, the corridors of power in Beijing.

With Goldman as advisor we began meeting with investors. Heidi Ueberroth, global president and my direct boss at the time, took over as the project lead while I served as the main presenter of the existing China business during the meetings. The investment proposal, selling 11% of NBA China for $253 million, generated strong interest and over-subscription from a wide range of investors. The ESPN division of Disney took 5%, but the rest of the offering was taken up by blue-chip Chinese investors who would tick the "strategic" and "*guanxi*" boxes: Bank of China, China Merchants Bank, Legend Holdings (main owner of Lenovo), and the Li Ka Shing Foundation.

In 2003, the NBA's China business consisted of a couple of people in the Beijing office and me commuting from Hong Kong. Annual revenues were in the low seven figures. By 2008, we had grown to an 80-person strong team across offices in Beijing and Shanghai, revenues in the high eight figures, outstanding profitability, and a $2.3 billion valuation.

Doing business in China, particularly for a relatively new product or nascent industry, requires substantial persistence, internal and external education, creative deal-making, and innovative company staffing and structuring. International companies also need to be prepared to ramp up very quickly in China once their product gains acceptance, given the market's exceptional size and momentum. As the Harvard Business Review once put it, "foreign executives must be adept at reworking management orthodoxies in real time if they're to do well in China."[4]

The Empire Strikes Back

With the NBA's growing profile in China, the question of face became even more important. We needed to walk some fine lines in our dealings with various government entities, especially the China Basketball Association (CBA).

The CBA is a subsidiary of the General Administration of Sports (GAS), a powerful entity that we carefully cultivated through official meetings with our top New York executives in tow, complemented by more casual meals and conversations over tea. All this took time, but

---

[4] Harvard Business Review magazine article, June 2010, *The Globe: The China Rules*, by Lynn S. Paine.

eventually we managed to develop cordial relationships with most of the key officials, at least at the GAS and their provincial arms in the key municipalities of Beijing, Shanghai, and Guangzhou.

The CBA proved more difficult. Around the year 2000, we met with CBA general secretary Xin Lancheng, a Communist Party stalwart from the Northeast of China, a region generally seen as more traditional and one of the slowest to reform during the last few decades of opening across the nation. He presented key challenges to the eventual ascension of Chinese players like Wang and Yao to the NBA.

In order to secure the release of Wang and Yao, we argued that having Chinese players in the NBA would benefit the CBA by honing their skills. China's national team would no doubt improve, sparking greater interest in basketball across the country. Mr. Xin refused, claiming the players would develop "bad habits" from the NBA, a risk that outweighed any potential benefits (A friend later told me that CCP members are taught in their party training schools to keep saying "no" in negotiations until they get what they want).

Eventually, Mr. Xin was replaced, and we saw a new opportunity. In 2003, Li Yuanwei took over as CBA general secretary. Although older than Xin, Li appeared more reform-minded and open to working with us. We managed to conduct joint player clinics and a week-long NBA-CBA Coaches Clinic (sponsored by McDonald's). The CBA agreed to allow us to use its name and endorsement, and bring local coaches and students to each program. The NBA flew in American coaches and players, and handled all other event operations, including sponsorship arrangements.

The deal was lopsided, but we accepted it as an investment in the relationship. We needed to be seen working with the Chinese government on growing the game and building the community in China. Joint events helped forge a closer working relationship with the CBA, our official window to the Chinese government. The events were well produced and ticked these boxes accordingly.

However, the good vibes from our initial collaborations did not last long. The next venture we sought the CBA's support for would be our biggest yet, the aforementioned 2004 NBA China Games. Under Chinese regulations, sporting events require official permission from the appropriate Chinese government entity, which for us was the CBA. We went into discussions with the CBA assuming the Games would grow basketball in China—ostensibly one of CBA's core missions—and that Secretary

Li would be happy to help smooth the way. To our surprise, we met resistance. After considerable back-and-forth, the CBA unveiled their bottom line: they would sanction the Games in return for a fee of one million RMB (about US$150,000).

The sum was modest compared to the high cost of bringing two NBA teams, plus equipment (we had to import our own floors, for example), and hundreds of support staff required to produce the games. To our league management, however, the actual expense was less the issue than the principle of it all. We would give CBA branding and credit well beyond the scope of their work and contribution, which basically amounted to a stamp of approval.

In our view, we deserved the CBA's support. Our investment was huge, and the CBA should be grateful for the impact the Games would have on our mutual goal of building the sport of basketball in China. So rather than give in and pay the sanction fee, regardless of the amount, we started looking for alternative sources for the approvals we needed.

The municipal sports administrations of Beijing and Shanghai were happy to oblige. Each of these government entities—technically on the same level as CBA in that they also reported directly to the central government's GAS—were not only willing to provide the requisite government approvals, but also pay a seven-figure ticket guarantee and provide the venue and security in each city. The municipal-level officials were eager to bring major events to their respective cities and receive credit for doing so. They understood the economic benefits and would gain huge face with official hosting responsibilities.

Our discussions with the municipalities were a breath of fresh air compared to our dealings with the CBA, even though the latter was technically the most appropriate partner. We moved forward with the two city governments accordingly.

The CBA leaders were furious. They viewed anything to do with basketball as their prerogative alone, and a sanction fee was simply standard procedure. As the CBA saw it, they had spent decades building up the sport of basketball in China. Foreigners coming in would grow the market, they understood, but the newcomers should pay their fair share. The NBA's circumvention went against this principle and the CBA's positioning in the government hierarchy. Li expressed his displeasure in various ways, including rejecting our invitations to attend the China Games launch press conference and other events as a VIP guest.

For everyone else, the 2004 NBA China Games were a huge success. The CBA continued to benefit from the NBA's work growing the sport's popularity in China. Relations remained cordial, although moving forward it was difficult to conduct joint programs with objectives and terms that satisfied both sides. This did not come as a big surprise. The NBA and CBA were and are both proud entities, as are their respective countries, with both requiring effective control over any initiatives held under their names.

From our viewpoint, we could not afford the risk of the CBA holding us back by bringing them closer. The CBA simply did not have the wherewithal to add value to NBA's China marketing machine, which was excelling on its own. We were in the heat of an exploding market with a business growing at a frenetic pace. We knew our end runs might upset the officials, but that was a risk we were willing to take in order to achieve our goals.

International companies in virtually every industry need to work with government partners in China, or at least to give an effort and the appearance of doing so, and build those relationships accordingly. However, it is often possible and sometimes necessary for foreign companies to conduct business in China with relatively little government involvement or help. It can also be beneficial to work with government entities that are tangential to those ostensibly having responsibility for one's particular industry, even if such end-arounds may annoy the responsible entity. All companies having or seeking a significant profile in China need to navigate government relations and the various dilemmas that may stem from them.

MEDALS ABOVE ALL

The 2008 Summer Olympics in Beijing, as with most editions of the quadrennial global spectacle, were more than just a sporting event. The games were in many ways China's coming-out party. China had accomplished tremendous economic and political reform after decades of isolation and poverty, and the Games were Beijing's chance to show the world how far it had come. In addition to the shiny new Olympic venues, the capital city completed many new buildings designed by top international architects, along with new transport systems and other facelifts throughout the city, all just in time to host visitors from around the world.

To ensure blue skies during the games, automotive traffic was rationed, and factories within a 100-mile radius of the capital were shut for weeks.

Special lanes were set up for Olympic transport. Thousands of smiling volunteers were enlisted. The Opening Ceremony, directed by famous Chinese moviemaker Zhang Yimou, was considered the grandest and most elaborate ever produced.

It wasn't just the hosting of the Olympic Games, both in the summer of 2008 and winter of 2022 that China saw as building up the nation's face internationally. To drive both patriotism domestically and an image of strength (or "soft power") globally, Beijing also sought to dominate the medals table.

"We must resolutely ensure we are first in gold medals," said Gou Zhongwen, the head of the Chinese Olympic Committee, on the eve of the 2020 Tokyo Olympics. As Hannah Beech of the *New York Times* remarked, "China's sports assembly line is designed for one purpose: churning out gold medals for the glory of the nation. Silver and bronze barely count. By fielding 413 athletes in Tokyo, the largest number since the Beijing Games in 2008, China aims to land at the top of the gold medal count — even if the Chinese public is increasingly wary of the sacrifices made by individual athletes."[5]

The government has set up a substantial national infrastructure to achieve their medal goals, largely following the Soviet sports model of hand-picking high-potential athletes at a young age and training them in specialized sports institutes that teach little more than the particular sports themselves. This commitment has in fact resulted in a large Olympic medal haul for China in numerous individual sports, such as gymnastics, diving, ping-pong, archery, weightlifting, and more recently individual snow and ski sports in the Beijing 2022 Winter Games.

China finished second to the United States in the overall and gold medals tables in Tokyo 2020, Rio 2016, and London 2012, and won the overall medal count at the Beijing 2008 Games (although still second to the Americans in the gold medal count). Not bad for a country that boycotted the Games from 1956 until 1984 due to Taiwan's participation, and battled with poverty and even starvation until the late 1970s.

---

[5] New York Times article, July 29, 2021, *China's Olympic Goal: The Most Golds, at Any Cost*, by Hannah Beech.

THE PROBLEM WITH TEAM SPORTS

Over the course of many Olympic games, China has won a total of 711 medals. But only 2% of that extraordinary haul came in large team events, and not a single one from a Chinese men's team. Amazingly, with a couple notable exceptions coming from strong women's volleyball teams, the nation of 1.3 billion people has consistently failed to produce internationally competitive entrants in large team sports, including the two most popular sports in the country and globally, football (soccer) and basketball.[6] There are several apparent reasons for the discrepancy between the popularity of major team sports and China's poor medal performance in this category.

First, Olympic medal tables count a medal for an individual the same as for a team. But building a winning team has proven harder for the Chinese system, in which individuals can be hand-picked at a young age based on size and other traits, then trained in specialized state-run sports institutions. This process does not work as well for team sports, which require a much larger pool of talent than such hand-picking can achieve. Competitive teams are created by starting with a large pool that is gradually improved and winnowed through increasingly stringent team practices and competitions. Culturally, Chinese parents rank sports low in priority, so a broad pool of sports talent was never established, despite the huge population. Unlike in the United States, Chinese kids tend not to play team sports after school or on weekends, which are spent studying for exams.

For similar reasons, China does not have enough qualified coaches for competitive teams at the professional and national levels. Even, the Chinese national and professional teams in major sports have been compelled to hire foreign coaches and trainers over the past dozen plus years.

---

[6] China's poor performance in team sports comes despite having hosted the two Olympics, FIBA Men's Basketball World Cup in 2019, and an expressed desire to host the FIFA Football World Cup—all of which require the host nation to field reasonably competitive teams in their underlying major team sports. Ironically, football (soccer) and basketball are China's most popular sports. A 2021 Nielsen survey of 8000 Chinese in tier 1–3 cities ages 16–69 showed basketball as the most popular sport overall, with 57% interest among those surveyed, and NBA (46%) and CBA (39%) as the most popular annually held sports leagues. Soccer followed closely with a general interest level of 49% of the surveyed urban population, with international football's English Premier League the top annually held competition.

Second, at least until just recently, China has lacked adequate facilities for team sports. The central government is addressing this shortfall, but the quality and quantity of new basketball and soccer facilities have been unevenly distributed. Many of the new facilities are privately owned and set up as businesses that charge fees that are unaffordable for many families who otherwise might have sent their kids to play there.

Third, there are aspects of Chinese society that encourage individual performance over teamwork. According to Simon Chadwick, Director of Eurasian Sport at Em Lyon Business school, "Contrary to popular opinion, China is a very individualistic society where the success of individual people within individual families is much more important very often than collective well-being."[7] This may come as a surprise to those who think that centuries of Confucianism, plus decades of Communism and socialist policies, has encouraged collectivism. In some ways, the opposite has occurred. The state's control over many aspects of people's lives, including how many children to produce, compels Chinese citizens to become even more focused on their own personal identity and individual achievements.

China's one-child policy, instituted in 1980 and enforced until circa 2016, has created generations of kids with no siblings. Children from large families have more opportunities to cooperate and share, which are critical skills in a team environment. Sports like basketball and soccer depend on teamwork both on and off the field. A player who is more concerned about individual performance will miss opportunities when passing is the better option for the team.

China's educational system is similarly optimized for individual performance, with its tendency toward rote learning. From an early age, students are taught to memorize correct answers rather than raise questions or think of alternative theories or independent ideas. Sports training in China follows a similar pattern. This system works well for math, and for learning thousands of Chinese characters, and it produces high-performing athletes in gymnastics, diving, weightlifting, shooting, and archery. It works poorly for team sports that require spontaneous creativity, problem-solving, and independent decision-making that involve other players. Thus, as the New York Times' Beech writes, "Beijing's

[7] Indian Express article, March 15, 2021, *Football Needs to be Far Less a State Instrument in China*, by Shivani Naik.

focus has been on sports that can be perfected with rote routines, rather than those that involve an unpredictable interplay of multiple athletes."[8]

China's generally poor performance at popular team sports has interesting implications for business. After all, what are companies if not teams of people? If China cannot field winning national teams from the world's largest population, how can managers build winning teams of staff?

In China, incentives still need to be individualized. Chinese staff will strive to hit team goals, only as long as they see a specific return for them personally in the achievement. My own process was to apply a three-part bonus system, with territory, department, and individual goals.

Managers should not expect most Chinese to have as much creative or problem-solving initiative of their own, relative to their Western counterparts. However, when Chinese staff are given specific enough training and other directions to follow for a project, along with the above incentives, they will work diligently until the task is done.

Baseball, America's favorite pastime, is the one Olympic team sport that China culturally has a good chance to excel at over time. The sport's core dynamic is more individualistic than other team sports due to the one-on-one battle between hitter and pitcher. Plays tend to be scripted in baseball and thus can be rehearsed by rote preparation, without the sort of spontaneous ball-passing required by other team sports. China's largest rivals in East Asia—Japan, South Korea, and Taiwan—all excel at baseball, providing ample incentive for China to catch up. Major League Baseball (MLB) has invested in a Beijing office, academies, and other grassroots programs in China over the past 15 years. The results are starting to bear fruit, with several promising Chinese prospects at the elite level and a rapidly growing base of young players.

BEIJING'S HEAVY HAND

Yan Qiang, the journalist who explained to me that "China is an anti-sports nation" was right about the traditional proclivity of Chinese people to focus on more ostensibly pragmatic interests, but the China sporting

---

[8] New York Times article, July 29, 2021, *China's Olympic Goal: The Most Golds, at Any Cost*, by Hannah Beech

scene has in fact improved markedly since 2009. President Xi Jinping is a big soccer fan and has voiced support for mixed martial arts (MMA) as a way of making Chinese people tougher. The central government's "Policy 46" launched in 2014, and further refined since then, has provided explicit and implicit incentives to encourage the growth of the nation's sports industry, with a financial goal for the sector to hit at least five trillion RMB (about US$720 billion) in total revenue by 2025.

Participation in a variety of sports has improved markedly as a result, the "athleisure" lifestyle has become fashionable, and various sports apparel and shoe brands—especially Chinese players such as Li-Ning and Anta—along with fitness clubs, youth training centers, and apps have experienced exponential growth.

Major global and domestic sports properties like the NBA and European football (soccer) also benefited from the boom, with digital media behemoths such as Tencent and Alibaba (along with the now bankrupt LeSports and PPTV) setting up huge sports arms and bidding hundreds of millions for league and event content rights. Non-sports brands seeking to tap into consumers' passions in new ways considered sports marketing options for the first time. Provincial and municipal governments invested in their own new sports programs, facilities, events, and tax incentives to keep in step with central government policy. Agencies large and small, such as my own Shanghai-based marketing consultancy, also experienced a slew of growth opportunities as a result of Policy 46, at least during the 2015–2020 period.

However, such major policy initiatives and grand event plans from the Olympics on down notwithstanding, the heavy hand of the government has arguably done as much to hold back the sustainable development of sports in China as it has to promote it. For example, as described above, the decades-long focus of the central sports administration on training individual athletes to capture a maximum of gold medals, rather than enabling broad-based participation at grass-roots levels. Meanwhile, buffeted by broad COVID-19 shutdowns, cancelations, and other restrictions, China's sports industry has come crashing back to earth after the first few years of wild investment promoted by the 2014 policy. It almost seems as if the government, and by extension the people, has viewed sports more as a means to achieve more traditional ends, such as patriotism or economic growth, as opposed to their intrinsic benefits such as health and teamwork.

The Chinese government's deep involvement in sports has at times held back individual athletes as well. Li Na, China's most accomplished tennis player of all time, showed early promise, but she struggled under Chinese Tennis Association (CTA) appointed coaches. She considered them to be both insufficiently skilled and too domineering (even forcing her to take steroids at one point), and in 2008 she finally quit the national team and left the state-run sports system entirely. She was allowed to do so under an experimental reform policy for tennis players, called *dān fēi* (单 飞), or Fly Solo. As a result, Li was allowed to hire her own coaching staff and keep more of her winnings, with only twelve percent going to the CTA development fund as opposed to sixty-five percent previously.[9,10]

The move out from under the national sports system paid off soon thereafter. Li Na became the first player representing an Asian country to appear in a Grand Slam singles final, finishing as the runner-up at the 2011 Australian Open, and then became the first Grand Slam singles champion from Asia, male or female, by winning the 2011 French Open. She then won the singles title at the 2014 Australian Open, achieving a career-high WTA ranking of world number two in February 2014.

In 2019, Li Na was inducted into the International Tennis Hall of Fame. As Beech reported for *Time* magazine in 2014, "To think that just six years ago, she was little more than a pawn of the Chinese state, a burned-out, injury-plagued athlete on the brink of retirement. Only a break from the sports machine that created her would save Li and transform her into a Chinese – and global – icon."[11]

The state has complete control over the media in China, giving it the ability to shape how people think about sports. The government has the ability to build support for its major sports initiatives such as Policy 46, the Olympics, and its national sports programs. Almost as significantly, the government uses its control of media to both build and to feed off the public's national pride in its winning athletes.

By the same token, Chinese media can be merciless in heaping criticism on its sports losers, or those it deems could in some way hurt national

[9] Wikipedia: https://en.wikipedia.org/wiki/Li_Na.

[10] In the summer of 2012, the required contribution to the Chinese tennis development fund was lifted and Li kept all her prize money.

[11] Beech, Hannah (2014), The Meaning of Li Na, Time, vo. 183, no.20, Asia-South Pacific Edition https://time.com/magazine/south-pacific/100613/may-26th-2014-vol-183-no-20-asia-south-pacific/

pride, and enables netizens to follow suit on social media. Partly for face and partly due to the government's propaganda regime, China is quick to love a winner and shun a loser. The media is all too ready to keep the masses fired up, one way or the other. One aforementioned example of this is the contrast between the admiring coverage of Yao Ming on the one hand, and the government led scorn of Wang Zhizhi on the other.

A more recent phenomenon was the adulation of freestyle skier Eileen Gu. Born and raised in San Francisco with a Chinese mother and (apparently estranged) American father, Gu decided in 2019 to compete for China and not the United States in the 2022 Beijing Winter Olympics. This proved to be a smart decision for the dominant skier and rising supermodel. The Chinese government, media, and public welcomed her with open arms, with messaging that implied her decision to compete for her mother's country was a high-profile example of the rise of emerging China and the decline of America.

At the same time, Gu and her mother carefully curated her image to avoid any political controversy surrounding her dual national identity. Gu's stock response on the matter has been consistently diplomatic: "When I'm in the US, I'm American, but when I'm in China, I'm Chinese." And as she wrote in Chinese on Weibo, China's Twitter equivalent, "I hope that through my pursuit of the extreme sport, I could enhance interaction, understanding and friendship between the Chinese and American people."

Gu quickly became the most popular 2022 Olympics competitor in China, bringing her millions of dollars in pre-Olympic endorsements ranging from Louis Vuitton to a dozen Chinese brands. And fortunately for Gu, she ended up winning two gold and one silver medal on the slopes of Beijing, contributing mightily to both her adoring media coverage and social media following, as well as her business opportunities, in China. After her first gold, CNN reported, "adulation for Gu literally crashed China's largest social media platform, as tens of millions rushed to celebrate her victory online."[12]

It is unclear, however, whether Gu's treatment in the Chinese media would have been so positive had she not won. Her fellow American-born Chinese athlete Zhu Yi, who also chose to compete for China instead of the United States, suffered intense cyberbullying on Chinese social media

---

[12] CNN article, February 12, 2022, *Fame and Fury: China's Wildly Different Reactions to US-Born Olympians*, by CNN staff.

after recording two falls in the team figure skating competition. Zhu's falls were blamed for causing the Chinese team to lose their medal chance in that particular competition. She also failed to win an individual medal in her later performance. Some commentators say it wasn't just the losses that unleashed such criticism for Zhu in China, but also the fact that she was "not Chinese enough." Zhu was apparently insufficiently fluent to hold interviews in Chinese prior to the Winter Games, in contrast to Gu who spoke fluently and even with a Beijing accent.

Just One Tweet

In October of 2019, the NBA's China business suffered a devastating blow. Daryl Morey, then general manager of the Houston Rockets, expressed support for pro-democracy protests by tweeting a message urging his followers to "stand with Hong Kong." Although quickly deleted, the tweet prompted an immediate backlash from Chinese social-media users, who targeted his account with calls for him to be fired. Official Chinese media released vicious editorials criticizing not only Morey and the Rockets but the NBA as a whole, defending the country's sovereignty against all forms of external interference. The timing could not have been worse, with the NBA about to stage a series of sold-out exhibition games in Japan and China.

Several days after the tweet, NBA headquarters tried to mitigate the damage by covering both the Chinese and American sides of the issue. In a prepared statement, the league clarified that Morey's support for Hong Kong protesters "does not represent the Rockets or the NBA," and that it was "regrettable" that Morey's tweet offended fans in mainland China, but it also noted that the NBA values the right of employees to weigh in on "matters important to them." The Chinese translation of the statement was worded to be somewhat more appeasing to China than the original English version.

Despite the league's middle-of-the-road approach, the response from China was harsh and unambiguous. Chinese media criticism of the tweet and the NBA's response was unrelenting. In the days following, the CBA and the bulk of the NBA's China business partners all cut ties with the Rockets and the league. Even Yao Ming, who had taken over the head job at the CBA several years earlier, joined the chorus of criticism. CCTV-5 banned all NBA broadcasts indefinitely.

China's reaction came as no surprise to those of us on the ground. For reasons related to national pride and history dating back to hundreds of years of suffering foreign incursions and submissions, the Chinese are remarkably sensitive to any perceived foreign interference on matters of territorial jurisdiction. Brooklyn Nets owner Joe Tsai explained why territory is a "third-rail issue" for the Chinese in his open letter to fans: "I am going into all of this because a student of history will understand that the Chinese psyche has heavy baggage when it comes to any threat, foreign or domestic, to carve up Chinese territories."[13]

I have seen time and again how extremely intelligent, Western-educated Chinese in high-level positions who are articulate and worldly in a wide range of topics, will revert to their nation's patriotic line when it comes to issues of sovereignty vis-a-vis places such as Tibet, Xinjiang, Taiwan, and Hong Kong.

Morey's tweet on Hong Kong certainly ticked the "interference" box, even though he was just one person, and ostensibly represented only himself with his tweet. Morey was a relatively well-known personality in China, due to his management role in China's most popular team. Therefore, his tweet mattered to the Chinese, and by association represented not only the Houston Rockets but the NBA as a whole.

Again, the reaction in China was predictable, but I was surprised by the NBA's not only delayed but ambivalent response. I had long since left the organization, but know that Adam Silver, like Stern before him, is a brilliant NBA commissioner and savvy leader, with a strong record of handling thorny situations decisively. His all but too careful response in this case was thus yet another example of the tightrope that multinational brands must walk between their constituents in China and those at home.

The NBA's public statements appeared to satisfy few of their intended audience on either side. A better tactic may have been for Silver to get on the next plane from Tokyo (where he happened to be overseeing exhibition games) to Beijing immediately following the tweet. The Chinese place great emphasis on personal contact. A visit to the capital and senior Chinese officials would give them face and may well have headed off the controversy before the criticism got picked up and amplified by official government media and high-profile spokespersons like Yao Ming.

---

[13] https://www.facebook.com/100001583307192/posts/2653378931391524?sfns=mo.

The heated criticism in the United States was also remarkable. People from both sides of America's political spectrum skewered the NBA for taking a position that seemed sympathetic to authoritarian China and lambasted Joe Tsai for trying to explain Beijing's position.

Even star players like Lebron James weighed in on the controversy, tweeting that Daryl Morey could have given more careful consideration to all sides of the issue, including the potential effects of such an inflammatory tweet from someone in his position. Like Tsai, James was vilified by many in the West for his rather moderate comments on the issue.

China's delicate political situation presents a challenge for any executive who wants to participate in China's vast market, but also believes in the principles of freedom and the right to free speech. Where does that right stop, and the responsibility to moderate one's public statements begin, especially for a high-profile executive like Morey? This is really the question that Lebron was asking, which I agree is a valid one. Did Morey fully understand and think through the potential effects of his tweet before he posted it? Some pundits argue that the controversy over his tweet actually accelerated China's tightening of control over the territory.

Meanwhile, nobody foresaw how much business would be lost from the quickly-deleted post.

In the three years since the October 2019 tweet, the NBA has scarcely appeared on CCTV or any other major regional TV channel in China. In response to government pressure, media backlash, and public sentiment against the NBA, most of the league's Chinese brand partners either terminated or did not renew their licensing agreements with the league.

That single tweet thus reportedly cut annual revenues in half for NBA China, from $400 million to $200 million within a year. The Houston Rockets alone lost $20 million in annual revenue from the China market due to the controversy. My own consulting business in Shanghai, which included advisory deals with a couple of those leading Chinese sponsors, lost about half of its business as well, almost overnight. Fortunately, our respective businesses have largely recovered, but a great deal of momentum was lost from the whole affair.

The Chinese government's heavy hand, as well as over-arching policies, can both give and take away. Doing business in China requires an ongoing awareness of government involvement and political sensitivities, and preparation to take advantage of favorable policies while at the same time staying nimble to adapt to any adverse changes.

Covid-19, and China's "zero-Covid" policy of containment, dealt a staggering blow to much of the China sports industry. Beginning in early 2020, professional leagues like the CBA and China Super League (CSL, the top pro soccer league) were forced to cancel large parts of their schedules and eventually play their seasons in "bubble" scenarios. The CSL fell into a particular state of disarray, with many clubs declaring bankruptcy over the past two years.

China, with its huge economy and growing affinity to sports and entertainment, had over the decade prior to Covid become an attractive destination for a long list of major global events like the HSBC world golf championship and the ATP tennis masters. All of these events were wiped off the calendar, either canceled entirely or moved to more open destinations by 2021. The 2022 Beijing Olympics ended up going ahead, but with extreme restrictions that limited fan attendance and on-ground activation.

The government showed its heavy hand with wide-ranging zero-Covid directives and enforcement. Besides eliminating most events on the domestic sports calendar for more than two years, these policies have impacted the economy on a massive scale. Instead of approving foreign mRNA vaccines soon after their certifications in the West and applying their power to compel all citizens (especially the elderly) to take them, Beijing insisted on using only less effective, locally developed vaccines.

Beijing instead put in place strict restrictions on travel, lockdowns, and confinement of anyone in the country who was exposed to the virus. After testing positive upon arrival at the Pudong airport, I spent all of January 2022 in an isolated Covid hospital in the outskirts of Shanghai, despite showing no symptoms of any illness. That was followed by another two weeks in a quarantine hotel room. Just six weeks later my family and I spent almost all of April and May locked in our apartment compound. Stories like this and worse have repeated themselves all over China. In fairness, China's lockdowns ostensibly stemmed the spread of the virus, and in doing so saved lives, at least in the short term. They certainly saved its medical systems from getting overwhelmed. On the other hand, the policies have dealt a major blow to both the country's economy and its reputation for pragmatism. Many foreign executives and their families have left China as a result. I was planning to leave Shanghai anyway, but the zero-Covid policy accelerated my timeline.

CHINA'S TRIBAL INSTINCTS

The reaction to any sort of foreign interference can be fueled by the tribalism that pervades Chinese society. When foreigners are involved in a conflict, Chinese people—often orchestrated behind the scenes by the government—are quick to unite as one tribe in an "us versus the outsiders" dynamic. This spills into sports competitions as well as in rallying around Olympic gold medal performances as a source of national pride.

The Asia Football Confederation has benefited from the intense rivalries between the China side and those of East Asian rivals Japan and Korea, as well as the club championships featuring professional teams from cities within those countries. Games between these rivals are always played in sold-out stadiums and in front of large live TV audiences.

The tendency for Chinese referees to favor local teams and players versus visiting teams, and especially foreign players, is legendary. The major professional leagues like CBA and CSL have been compelled, by both their global governing bodies as well as fans and media, to add foreign referees in response to protests of such bias. Over the years, there have been numerous ugly incidents involving foreign players and unfair treatment. Players who protested or complained about unfair treatment were showered with verbal abuse or objects thrown from the local audience during and after their games. Such incidents have led Chinese authorities to require at least 10%, and often 20%, of the audience seats to be filled by police or soldiers whose main responsibility is crowd control.

In recent years, China's domestic sports brands have exploited the people's tribal instincts and resulting nationalistic tendencies to drive sales and increase market share. Nike has seen growth of over 300% in China during the past decade but now, Chinese brands like Anta and Li-Ning are rapidly gaining strength, with Anta surpassing Nike sales in the first half of 2022. Political considerations seem to be playing a role. As reported by Front Office Sports, "In March 2021, Nike and other foreign brands made public statements denouncing the use of cotton produced from western Xinjiang region of China due to human rights violations. The result? Backlash from the Chinese population."[14]

As we have seen from the government down to its consumers, China will not tolerate such criticism from foreign entities. The FOS report continues, "This is when the data shifts. After the Xinjiang protests by brands, Bloomberg reported that Anta, Li-Ning, and Xtep quickly took the top three spots in terms of sales. Ever since that moment, the Fujian Tigers (a nickname for Chinese sportswear companies) have anchored themselves to the top of the sales list—gaining incremental benefits from events like the Winter Olympics in Beijing....by the end of January 2022, Anta and Li-Ning accounted for 28% of sneaker sales, twelve percentage points higher than before the Xinjiang outcry. Over the 12-month period ending January 31, domestic Chinese brands saw sales grow by 17% while foreign brands saw sales decline by 24%."

Ironically, Nike initially built its business in China by associating closely with the NBA and foreign sports stars and continued to position its brand for years as the global leader and thus aspirational choice. But the swift reaction of Chinese consumers, voting with their wallets, sent the global giant scrambling to position itself as less of a foreign brand in China. CEO John Donahue even stated in a June 2021 analyst call that Nike is a "brand of China and for China."

The above shift from foreign to domestic in sports brands seems to be taking place across many industry sectors in China. The government has not had to launch a huge "Buy Chinese" campaign to promote this (recalling the "Buy American" campaign in the United States), for several reasons. One is that domestic product quality and brand marketing have increased swiftly over the past decade. A second is that the Chinese themselves, quite practically, see globalism declining, with more barriers to China's exports, and thus, the need to support their own brands to keep more money in China.

The decline of "brand America" has also played a role. The United States, once looked up to as a shining beacon of quality and aspiration, is now seen more as a divided, decaying, China-bashing nation. No wonder a recent NBA China executive stated that "NBA is no longer an American brand, it's a global brand."

---

[14] https://frontofficesports.com/nike-nationalism-and-the-new-paradigm/ Front Office Sports article, February 20, 2022, *Nike, Nationalism, and the New Paradigm*, by Liam Killingstad.

Chinese tribalism binds people with common bonds and backgrounds in competition against those who are perceived as "others." Foreign businesspeople in China need to be aware of this dynamic when building their management teams, and relating to government. Understanding how tribalism works in China can help avoid pitfalls, but it can be used to advantage as well. It remains to be seen how foreign brands will perform, given the increasing trend to "buy Chinese." Brands will need to innovate and to some extent localize, while staying authentic to their brand DNA, in order to stay attractive to Chinese consumers.

> Cheating, and the question of how Chinese and Western cultures diverge on the subject of what passes for "honesty," is hotly debated. It would be difficult to say if cheating takes place more in one culture or another, but scholars have pointed out that the West is a guilt-based culture, whereas China puts more emphasis on blame and shame. Thus in China, there may be cheating or lying to gain an advantage—on or off the field—but it's getting caught that creates the real problem. Chinese soccer has a history of controversy involving match-fixing by coaches, players, and referees, and in 2009 a high-profile crackdown on corruption in the sport led to dozens of arrests and prison sentences. China is not the only place where this has happened, but the country has not yet built a reputation for fair play.

Two Steps Forward

Despite the issues and challenges described in this chapter, China still has a lot to offer international sports businesses, and vice versa.

First is the sheer scale and growth of the market, which isn't going away, in our lifetimes at least. China has experienced a few setbacks in recent years but in my experience is a place where the expression "one step backwards, two steps forward" applies like no other. Massive gyrations of enormous progress followed by disasters of one kind or another have occurred throughout most of its history.

The sports industry is going through a "one step backwards" stage now after remarkable growth from 2016 to 2020, when the market doubled in size to achieve 3% of GDP. The pandemic has knocked the industry back since then. In 2020, the first year of COVID-19, China's total sports industry output decreased by 7.2% compared with 2019.[15] Recent years have seen a host of bankruptcies by local sports-related companies, as well as payment defaults on international IP licensing deals.

But like other industries in China, sports are adjusting to conditions for significant long-term growth. The government continues to study opportunities to loosen its grip and apply more free-market practices, including privatizing the major leagues and less restrictive approvals for on-ground events.

Over time, China should figure out how to do better at team sports too. Stemming again from Policy 46, all students of elementary and high school age are now required to play sports for at least one hour a day. Other recent laws that should free up more time for young people to play sports include weekly time limits on electronic gaming, and a national prohibition of private after-school tutoring companies. The government has funded 50,000 new soccer pitches since 2015. As part of a broader technological push, Beijing has also pushed innovation and digitalization of sports, encouraging sports businesses to partner with local academic institutes to set up R&D centers and leverage advanced technologies such as 5G, artificial intelligence, and big data.

Wisely, Beijing has encouraged ties between the sports industry and related sectors such as tourism and healthcare. For example, the southern province of Hainan strives to become a sports tourism destination by attracting a series of international sports events to the island. Meanwhile, a wide variety of businesses related to sports have been booming, such as sports medicine and rehab clinics, online and offline fitness clubs, and training equipment.

A few sectors even saw particularly strong growth during the pandemic. E-sports have major events without live audiences (so no COVID-19 impact), but huge online viewership. These continued to be held in China throughout the pandemic, building a total audience now estimated to be more than 400 million nationally. The turnover of China's e-sports market leads the world, increasing 25% year on year in 2019 to $17.4 billion, including PC client e-sports games, mobile e-sports games, as well as offline events, e-sports live streaming and sponsorship. The market reached $20.8 billion in 2020 and $24.5 billion in 2021 with growth spurred by e-sports tournaments and live streaming.

---

[15] Announcement on Total Scale and Value-added Data of National Sports Industry in 2020; National Bureau of Statistics of China, 2021-12-31.

Winter sports have gained momentum from Beijing's 2022 Olympic Games. According to the National Bureau of Statistics, more than 346 million Chinese people have participated in winter sports since 2015, enjoying activities like skating, skiing, and ice hockey. This exceeded the goal set by Xi Jinping that year to engage around a quarter of the population.

Annual sales of home-workout gear increased by more than 60% since the onset of the pandemic. This includes fitness machines connected fitness such as interactive mirrors and bikes, and miscellaneous pieces like yoga mats, skipping ropes, massage therapy "guns," and other such products. Smart wearable devices in the sports and fitness fields such as smart bracelets, smart running shoes, and smart sports watches have also developed rapidly.

Meanwhile, China's young adults appear quite open to adopting new sports, especially if they offer a social element for both men and women. Mixed martial arts and the Ultimate Fighting Championship (UFC) have enjoyed a boom in followers of both genders in the three years since Chinese fighter Zhang Weili won the women's Strawweight belt. China's top-tier cities have also seen the sport of Ultimate Frisbee surge at the grassroots level in the last few years, as editor Yan recently observed, "because it's a sport that both men and women can enjoy on mixed teams together. Women drive at least 70% of purchase decisions in China, and men follow the trends that women set. In China, when young women take to any type of exercise or sport, young men are quick to follow."

Overall, today almost 65% of Chinese urban residents consider themselves sports fans and more than 35% of them practice sports regularly.[16] China's government expects the latter figure to increase to 45% by 2035. So the past couple of years are more an aberration than a change of course of the large-scale growth of China's sports industry.

One way or the other, China will hit the annual sports industry turnover target of five trillion RMB (about US$720 billion) by 2025, and then set a new five-year target that will probably be at least double that. A good thing about the involvement of China's government is that everyone knows the goals, and when Beijing sets a goal it goes about getting it done without further debate standing in the way.

---

[16] Nielsen Fan Insights—China—2021.

Opportunities for international sports business, whether they are top international leagues or events, training, products, or agencies, will continue to grow commensurately. So we can conclude this first positive point with a profound contradiction: even in the face of deep-seated cultural habits, as noted above, China is in fact on its way to becoming a sports nation.

This long-term growth track feeds the second major positive for American or other international sports businesses seeking to grow opportunities in China: simply that China still needs the expertise and excellence of leading international practitioners throughout this industry. From large sports properties like NBA or EPL, all the way down to grassroots training, competition events and leagues, the West is still decades ahead of China. And sports are not so easy to reverse-engineer, like the physical products that make up the core of other industries. Sports are a people business where expertise is grown over years of practice and needs to be continually refined. One cannot become a good sports trainer simply by reading a manual, but rather by years of working with experts and athletes.

Leagues like the NBA have taken decades to establish their prominence, but now that they are on top have cornered the market on all the key competitive advantages, such as top talent, ample financing, arena rights, and fan bases who want to watch the world's best in that sport compete. Chinese practitioners may one day achieve the experience to replicate all that themselves, but it will take at least a couple more decades to catch up to that point. Meanwhile, they have no choice but to import professional talent to continue their progress in growing interest and excellence in sports.

The last but certainly not least important positive about China: the Chinese people. With a cultural character sprinkled with apparent contradictions, at least from a Western point of view, Chinese people are at their core friendly, industrious, practical, and entrepreneurial. They can be neglectful toward strangers, but make up for this shortfall by going to almost any length to help family, friends, or others with whom they feel they have some meaningful connection.

And they remain open, and in fact often quite keen, to make such connections with Westerners, including Americans, despite saber rattling and other such tensions between their government and Western countries. As such, by showing a reciprocal openness to Chinese people, including at least an attempt to learn and use Mandarin, foreigners like myself have had the chance to meet and befriend a wonderful range of incredible individuals throughout greater China.

Meanwhile, the entrepreneurial and competitive spirit of Chinese culture has given its people the habits, will, and ability to work extremely hard to achieve their goals, even when faced with what we in the West might see as debilitating obstacles. And the practical nature of the Chinese people, combined with their authoritarian model of governance, enables them to achieve both small and big things—for example, major construction projects—in less than half the time and budget that we may be accustomed to in the West.

This "can do" attitude means that adept business managers who set clear goals, and put in place training and incentives to achieve them, can achieve amazing results from their China teams. At the same time, international company executives in China need to stay aware and ahead of the various risks and challenges described in this chapter.

This brings to mind, in closing, my favorite expression about this fascinating country: "In China, anything is possible. But nothing is easy."

Mark Fischer   *is the former Managing Director of NBA China, and currently CEO of Fischer Sports & Entertainment. From 1997-2009, Fischer held a series of leadership roles at the National Basketball Association (NBA) in Asia, including as founding Managing Director of NBA China where he oversaw all business segments—media, marketing, brand partnerships, merchandise, and events—and led the territory's explosive growth from a two-man startup to a valuation of $2.3 billion. He went on to establish operations in Asia for the Ultimate Fighting Championship (UFC), during which time he drove more than 10-fold increases in both audience and revenues, organized UFC's first six events in the region, and produced a 12-episode Chinese version of the Ultimate Fighter reality show series. Mr. Fischer is currently the CEO of Fischer Sports & Entertainment, which provides advisory and business development services to help brands, rights-holders, and related entities harness the growing popularity of sports in Asia. Proficient in Mandarin, the Boston native holds a Master's degree in Public Administration from Harvard's Kennedy School of Government, and a Bachelor's in History from the University of Michigan.*

CHAPTER 8

China-U.S. Supply Chain: Pragmatic Relationships and Laissez-Faire

Daniel M. Krassenstein

Today's news cycle is dominated by the words "China" and "global supply chains," with complicated stories about congested ports and elevated freight rates. The current supply chain challenges, the situation in China, and what we can expect in the future, are some of the questions being raised. Did China deliberately cause the product shortages and the higher prices we pay for consumer goods? Is China part of the problem, the solution, or both? What are the pros and cons of America's decoupling from China and on-shoring, near-shoring, or alternative off-shoring production? How does the savvy multinational mitigate risks and manage the chaos? Can American companies build trusting relationships with their China counterparts in today's highly politicized business environment?

As an American supply chain specialist with over 20 years based in China, my work puts me at the center of these questions. I will attempt to demystify much of the complexity of these questions and share some of

D. M. Krassenstein (✉)
Global Supply Chain Director at Procon Pacific. Lombard IL, USA
e-mail: daniel.krassenstein@outlook.com

© The Author(s), under exclusive license to Springer Nature Singapore Pte Ltd. 2023
K. D. Gibbs (ed.), *Selling to China*,
https://doi.org/10.1007/978-981-99-1953-6_8

the lessons I've learned. Global trade, which is based on sound business values, is most efficient when there is little interference from politics. The focus should instead be on the value proposition—who is bringing what value (assets, skills, networks, intellectual property, raw materials, market access, etc.) into the relationship, quantifying that value, and identifying whether the business is sustainable and advantageous when compared to alternative sources, locations, and supply chain configurations. The value analysis is dynamic and most certainly will change over time.

The Root Cause of Today's Supply–Demand Imbalance

The goal of global supply chain management is to structure the international supply chain to maximize its competitive advantage and benefits to the consumer. Even in the best of times, with so many variables at play, it is a constant challenge to balance supply and demand and minimize waste. The COVID-19 pandemic caused America's demand for consumer goods—from home office furniture to home exercise equipment—to suddenly increase even beyond the most optimistic of forecasts. At the same time, many factories in China were forced to shut down in order to slow the spread of the pandemic. When these manufacturers returned to work, the pent-up volume waiting to be transported from China to the United States was unprecedented and far exceeded the available space aboard the container vessels. When this type of supply and demand imbalance occurs, costs increase.

The costs of operating a factory in China also increased substantially (due to higher salaries and COVID-19-compliance requirements in factories), while the cost of transportation (e.g., factory-to-port drayage and ocean freight rates) quintupled. In spite of these increased costs, demand for consumer goods remained strong; the net result of which is inflation. The root cause of the product shortages was China's government-mandated lockdown measures which constrained the supply side; this was exacerbated by huge increases in demand as the lockdowns in the United States shifted buyer behavior from services to goods. Additionally, this trade surge has exposed many infrastructure weaknesses in the United States—from inefficient maritime ports to insufficient warehousing, to bottlenecks in our rail and trucking industries. Consolidation among the larger ocean container carriers and an oligopolistic retail market (dominated by Amazon, Wal-Mart, and Target) have exacerbated these inefficiencies.

SUPPLY CHAIN SHIFTS HAPPEN

Production shifts are a normal and predictable occurrence. In the 1970s, production shifted from Japan to the four tigers (Taiwan, Korea, Hong Kong, and Singapore), then on to China in the 1990s. What has been unprecedented, however, has been how long China held onto its dominance of low-cost manufacturing. It has done so by having a very large workforce (scale) and world-class infrastructure, resulting in cost efficiencies. Stability in China's policy environment and pro-business orientation have also been important differentiators vis-a-vis other emerging market production locations. However, by 2015, China's labor costs had already increased to such a level that labor-intensive manufactured consumer goods (from clothing to footwear) had already started to shift from China to Southeast Asia (Vietnam) and South Asia (India and Bangladesh). What makes this production shift different is the large number of factories that have remained in China and continue to be profitable. The main reasons are automation in manufacturing—allowing China to remain competitive in certain industries—and an efficient and predictable logistics network. Another factor that has helped Chinese factories remain viable is their own domestic market. China's growing middle class is increasingly consuming the same type of items traditionally exported to the United States (automobiles, TVs, sports and leisure items, furniture, etc.).

On the other hand, the recent introduction of punitive duty tariffs on Chinese products (up to 25%) coupled with ocean freight costs increasing sixfold (from $3,000 to over $20,000) has resulted in American consumers having to pay significantly higher prices for consumer goods. One would think that this alone should be sufficient cause for even more of the manufacturing to shift out of China; however, it is not that simple. It takes time to scale up manufacturing capacity in other countries, as this requires investment not just in factory equipment, but in highways and port infrastructure as well. Furthermore, countries like Vietnam have grown their production capacity faster than the logistics infrastructure, resulting in severe congestion on the roads and ports. Also, Vietnam's labor rates have already increased to a level that erodes its own position as a low-cost leader for certain product segments.

Thus, global manufacturers with production facilities in China are now re-evaluating how to most efficiently satisfy consumer demand from three unique markets: (a) United States, (b) China, and (c) the rest of the world. What we are witnessing is a decline in the concentration of single large-scale manufacturing facilities in China (to meet the needs of the world's consumers), to smaller-scale plants satisfying local or regional demand. In certain commodity segments, it is becoming more cost-efficient to meet the needs of the American consumer from smaller-scale near-shore factories in Mexico or the Dominican Republic. Thus, when a multinational company is faced with a new capital investment decision for increased capacity, it is now less likely to do so in China. Instead, it converts that existing China facility to focus on the domestic market and the nearby markets of Japan and Korea and builds new facilities closer to the target market. Also, production is differentiated by category, with less-advanced manufacturing being more easily relocated.

VALUE-BASED RELATIONSHIPS DETERMINE SUSTAINABILITY

"Selling to China" is an easily misunderstood phrase, as it has the possibility to lead the reader to envision the foreigner as a traveling salesman, trying to sell goods, or services from a foreign land to satisfy the consumption appetite of the Chinese consumer. From a global supply chain practitioner's perspective, however, the concept takes on a broader meaning: How does a foreigner motivate a Chinese business to value them as part of their own global supply chain network? This forces the foreigner to perform a SWOT (Strength Weakness Opportunity and Threat) analysis to measure their own competitive value—i.e., what am I bringing of *value* to my potential Chinese stakeholders? It does not matter if you are a global buyer or a global seller. The Chinese business will simply look at you pragmatically and evaluate whether working with you is in their short-term best interest. I say short-term because neither party truly knows whether they will be compatible in the medium-term or long-term, so why pretend?

One of the key lessons I've learned from decades of doing business in China is to appreciate the frank pragmatism of the Chinese perspective. Don't be naive: It isn't personal, it's just business. If your Chinese partner can find a better way to satisfy their business objectives either on their own or with somebody else, then the onus is on you to either modify your approach or move on to your next opportunity.

FIRST IMPRESSIONS—SUPPLY RELATIONSHIPS IN CHINA

My career in Asia began in 1985 when I landed in Taipei with the romantic idea of becoming a global trader (likely influenced by reading too many James Clavell novels). However, in reality, I was a 21-year-old "fresh off the boat" American kid who quickly learned I was woefully under-prepared for the global business world. Sure, I was a university graduate and relatively street smart, but that did not even bring me to the starting gate. What "perceived value" did I bring to the party? Teaching English! This paid for my rent and Chinese-language classes, so I humbly accepted that initial role as I got myself established. Over time, I purposefully took on business-English teaching gigs, so I could network and learn more about Chinese business practices.

Bear in mind, this was the late 1980s, and to the then "adventurous American" Taiwan was where one went to learn Mandarin and how to work with the Chinese business culture. Mainland China (as we called the People's Republic of China back then) was a future with infinite potential, but not yet realistically approachable. At the time, Taiwan indeed was a global provider of low-cost light goods manufacturing. I found suppliers of familiar products (baseball caps, hardware tools, vinyl floor tiles, etc.) and filled my suitcases with samples on sales trips back to the United States. At each sales visit, I was met with an increasingly familiar uninterested potential buyer, as they also did not see value in me as an intermediary. The Taiwan factory did not value me as a buyer and the American buyer did not value me as a seller, which made for a humbling experience.

Two years later, I found a valuable niche. The adage of "the right place and the right product at the right price" proved to be true. A friend of my father, who was in the advertising promotional products industry, was looking for a supplier of pens with a pharmaceutical company's drug logo imprinted upon them as part of their promotional campaign. Being in Taiwan (right place) and knowing a suitable pen manufacturer (right product) allowed me to cut out several layers of middlemen (right price) and put me in the sweet spot of being valued by all parties. Finally, I had a compelling value proposition.

1990S—2020S SUPPLY CHAIN

In 1994, I moved to Shanghai with a Sino-British logistics firm to establish their marketing and sales departments. I spent the first several weeks just learning and observing existing practices and norms. The Chinese partners in the business were large state-owned enterprises, and they were resistant to my very presence. They did not like my pricing tariffs, which we needed to ensure our container trucks were profitable. They were even less happy that I would show up at Shanghai Port meetings where haulage assignments were being divvied out to the local trucking companies. That I spoke Mandarin and was experienced in the logistics industry made them feel threatened. When I reported to the British partner that our joint venture's profitability was not their Chinese partners' motivation, I was surprised to discover this was already well-known (and they were impressed by how quickly I'd figured it out!).

A memorable moment from that job was a year-end party where I was the sole foreigner out of 450 people in attendance. There was a karaoke microphone with an accompanying movie projector showing the Chinese characters to the song with a video background. The vice chairman of our company sang the Chinese song *"dōngfāng hóng"* (东方红) or "The East Is Red" and on the projector was shown an old black and white propaganda movie about Chinese soldiers supporting the North Koreans by killing Americans. As he sang the song louder and louder, he kept looking directly at me. The rest of my colleagues (with whom I had great rapport) shooed me to another room and told me to ignore him.

It took a while, but eventually I won over the Chinese partners, as I was able to find a valued niche that they appreciated. I dealt with our three main foreign customers (Volkswagen, H&M, and Mercantile (the then freight consolidation arm of Maersk). Those three multinational clients were happy that I could understand their wants and needs and resolve their issues. The more indispensable I became, the better the Chinese partners treated me—as long as I didn't interfere with their side hustles.

Our company had 82 Scania tractors hauling containers to and from the port of Shanghai. We had a Class A forwarder's license and two bonded warehouses. Our local partners were the who's who of the China logistics industry. Meanwhile, we constantly faced the challenge of unpredictable highway and bridge tolls that our drivers had to pay, especially in Zhejiang Province. Our drivers would come back from a typical Shanghai-Hangzhou-Shanghai haulage with toll receipts of sometimes ¥300 ($35) and other times over ¥1,500 ($180). The toll receipts were genuine. What we later learned was that there were competing government (local and provincial) authorities each claiming the right to assess tolls. Some of the toll stations were temporary, depending on their revenue needs.

Another challenge I encountered was in our own warehouses, where we would receive thousands of export cartons each day for the Swedish retailer, H&M. Some of the cartons were marked to go to Gothenburg, while others were for Stockholm. Unfortunately, our warehouse kept mixing up the cartons, forcing H&M Sweden to sort things out at the destination, and adding expense. After an internal review, I realized that our warehouse staff couldn't read the English shipping mark on the cartons. I resolved this by implementing a color-coding system where the factory would paint a blue square on each carton going to Gothenburg and a yellow square for those going to Stockholm, problem solved!

More recently, I had shipments originating in Sichuan that had to route via Shanghai to load onto the ocean container vessels. The logical lowest-cost route is via the Yangtze River, which flows almost 4,000 miles across China. However, halfway from Sichuan to Shanghai is the Three Gorges Dam, a frequent bottleneck for container ships. I came up with a workaround where we would truck from Sichuan to Yichang, Hubei (just east of the dam) to avoid the congestion, then load the container onto a barge from there to Shanghai. It cost a bit more than shipping only via the river, but far less than trucking the entire way. Even better, this method avoided any delays, another problem solved!

With respect to manufacturing, I am often impressed by how lean Chinese factories are. Frugality is a strong Chinese ethos. Resources are usually not wasted. That said, when I visit a factory with an extravagant entrance and fancy gardens, chandeliers, or other outlandish accouterments, I wonder who they are trying to impress—and why. Most of the Chinese suppliers I've worked with over the years are very good at subcontracting. They know where their internal strengths are (perhaps in communication with the overseas buyer, accounting, assembly, quality control, packing and shipping documents), but they also know which areas should be outsourced (raw material processing, plastic injection molds, trucking, freight forwarding, or even trade finance). It is for this reason that many of my suppliers tend to be located in tight geographic clusters, as they want to be near the material providers. The managing directors typically are very cost-focused and track everything carefully—down to each machine's utilization and units/worker of output per day.

Factory owners really do range from the caring and benevolent (perhaps providing housing for the workers' aging parents or paying school tuition for their kids) to the ones who dock workers' pay for slow work or quality mistakes. As in the West, there is no one single accurate description. One major difference is the factory ownership—either state-owned enterprise (SOE), privately-owned (including foreign-invested), or a combination of the two. The SOEs that I have dealt with have been professionally managed by well-educated bureaucrats. While they may strive for their own unit's profitability, many also know their unit's value to society—providing employment, social stability, and overall improvement to the community and quality of life. This may seem like propaganda in the context of a Western enterprise that answers primarily to shareholders, but I observed good results from this system. In the West, we may label this ESG (Environmental, Social, and Governance), but the objectives are essentially the same.

A final note on cooperating with Chinese factories—they are not inflexible. If I am able to prove to a factory manager that greater transparency and flexibility in their order processing would lead to better forecasting and increased orders, then they often do try to accommodate. If I am able to show the floor manager the benefits of maintaining a clean workshop (for quality certifications and for attracting new customers), they do want to learn and adapt. The key is to present the opportunity to them in a manner that appeals to their role and motivations.

LABOR AND MANAGEMENT OBSERVATIONS

The typical labor force of a factory in coastal China is primarily made up of domestic migrant workers, known as *wàidì rén* (外地人). Around Shanghai, many of these workers come from Anhui or Henan provinces. Mostly in their early twenties and coming from rural communities with limited education, these workers can earn a lot more money in the factories than they could at home. Factories generally provide room and board, but they expect employees to work 10–12 hour shifts for 6 days a week. Many of these workers see their families only once a year, at Chinese Year. The salaries for these workers have quintupled over the past 10 years, from ¥2,000/month ($300) to now over ¥10,000/month ($1,500).

The relationships between the managing directors and their direct reports can be quite interesting. In general, the more hands-on the leaders are, the better their middle-level managers are. The most effective leaders are those that literally walk the floor several times per day and know the names of most of their employees. Some of my most productive meetings have been when I've pointed out a deficiency in a Chinese factory. The boss will stop whatever they're doing and bring in his key staff for a review. Rarely are they defensive about their weaknesses; instead, they are eager to improve. I certainly conduct myself as a team player and try hard to avoid making anyone lose face, so my constructive criticisms are almost always well-received. As a customer, what more could I ask for? Over the years, the pendulum of power between the managers and the factory employees has swung in favor of the workers. Surprisingly, this has less to do with government intervention or public relations; this actually has more to do with supply and demand. Contrary to what an outsider would think, while China may have 1.4 billion citizens, its productive workforce (counted as those who are both skilled and willing to work 70 hours per week for $3–4/hour) has shrunk. Therefore, the manager not only has to behave considerately and respectfully to their workers, but he or she increasingly needs to provide nicer living quarters, better food, and even weekend entertainment. The competition from other factories for the shrinking workforce is intense. The factories essentially act as training centers to teach essential skills, then do their best to retain the most productive trainees.

A few years ago, as I noticed the Chinese worker labor cost increases, I conducted a comparative study (see chart) of China vs. Vietnam vs. India. I learned that, based on the monthly wage level, China was 70% higher than Vietnam and 300% higher than India. However, when the *productivity* of both the worker and the facility were factored in, the differences were significantly narrower—China's labor cost was only 11% higher than Vietnam's and 38% higher than India's. While this analysis was specific to my own labor-intensive industrial textile business, many of my peers on the supply chain committee of the American Chamber of Commerce in Shanghai confirmed that the comparisons generally held true in their industries as well (Table 8.1).

My observations of foreign-owned (especially American, German or Korean) factories in China offer comparative insight. Foreign-owned companies typically offer salaries about 20% higher than locally-owned factories, and the working conditions are generally better (temperature

Table 8.1 Labor cost comparison

	Vietnam	India	China
Monthly Wages	$475.00	$200.00	$800.00
Productivity	1.5	2.5	1.0
Equalized Wages	$712.50	$500.00	$800.00
Wages/Day	$23.75	$16.67	$26.67
Cost Per Unit	$0.79	$0.56	$0.89
Cost Comparison	−11%	−38%	0%

controlled, mandatory rest breaks, self-improvement training, safer work practices). In spite of that, the foreign-owned factories often have labor retention problems, as the locally-owned firms offer higher incentives to the trained staff coming from the foreign firms, given that they bring knowledge and know-how to their own businesses, clever! More recently, as patriotic fervor has increased on both sides of the Pacific, some of the perceived benefits from working for a foreign enterprise have diminished. It is not hard to imagine how conflicted a worker in a foreign-owned factory in China may feel as the relationship between the United States and China continues to deteriorate.

THE IMPORTANCE OF INFRASTRUCTURE

The importance of infrastructure in the global supply chain is often over-looked. China's coastal provinces have been export-focused for the past forty years. The provincial and national level authorities recognize the value of trade and have invested heavily in highways, railways, airports, and seaports—making them among the most modern and efficient in the world. As a result, the logistics costs to move Chinese products to the rest of the world are lower than in alternative manufacturing countries. Contrast China with manufacturing clusters in Vietnam, Bangladesh or India, and the differences are obvious. China has mostly resolved the power outages, flooded roads, and congested ports that can cause delays and bottlenecks. When calculating the all-in delivered cost of the product, these additional costs (both time and transport) are often as important as the cost of manufacturing.

Unit Labor Cost Productivity is measured as units produced divided by labor cost; however, that does not tell the whole story, merely the ex-works cost component. To tell the full story, one must calculate the door-to-door cost. A few years ago, I conducted a Lean Six Sigma Black Belt analysis on our India vs. China production and came to the realization that on certain lane segments, India was not really the lower-cost option. While Kolkata (in northeast India, close to Bangladesh) may offer lower absolute labor costs, that does not consider the time/cost expended to bring the container to the port, and the time/cost to then bring that container to the United States. In this example, Kolkata is an off-line origin that requires a feeder vessel to ship the container to a mainline hub to transship to a line-haul vessel that calls on the American port. The shipping costs are expensive and the overall transit time is longer, and often less dependable. Now, contrast that with sailing directly from Shanghai to Los Angeles in under two weeks with several vessels per week to ensure reliability and the comparison becomes a bit murkier.

The inefficiencies of America's infrastructure also add to the cost of products to the consumer. It is not uncommon to hear about 30–50 ships anchored outside of the congested ports of Southern California, New York, or Charleston. The bottlenecks are caused by insufficient capacity in the antiquated port, rail, highway and warehouse infrastructure. America's investment in modernizing its infrastructure would also go a long way to supporting its export products of agriculture and autos.

COMMERCIAL RELATIONSHIPS ARE CRITICAL TO SUCCESS

A commercial relationship is simply a relationship arising out of a trans-action process. However, when you add the complexities of international transactions involving different cultures, it becomes far more difficult to standardize what a good relationship looks like. The operative word is "relationship"—the way people are connected. The bond which exists between two people who have built trust and credibility has an inherent value.

After decades of doing business in China, I still maintain excellent relationships with dozens of factories. While the volume of orders I place in China today is lower than previously (shifted mostly to India), the commercial relationships are still based on solid foundations. I can approach any one of our China suppliers with a project opportunity and they will assess each one on its own merits. That the project is being presented by me, a trusted buyer, will ensure that project receives a proper review. My point is that the Chinese factories are pragmatic and look at business deals the same way an American would—a combination of credibility assessment and potential profits are the drivers. Nationalism and/or other external political factors rarely matter. It is just business.

CHINA MANUFACTURING FOR THE UNITED STATES, DOMESTIC MARKETS, AND THE REST OF THE WORLD

Twenty-five years ago, American companies typically entered into a China venture to take advantage of comparatively low labor costs. Today, however, China is no longer the low-cost producer, so that value proposition is no longer valid. As such, an American company with a capital investment already in China needs to analyze and reassess its reason for being there. While this analysis is industry and product specific, what many are discovering is that while China exporting to the United States may no longer be cost competitive, their existing plant may actually be competitive in selling to third countries (say, Korea or Australia), or even to the increasingly affluent and sophisticated China domestic market. The most profitable American manufacturers in China are mostly those that recognize this changing dynamic and focus their marketing efforts accordingly. We often hear the phrase, "In China, for China," which refers to foreign operations that produce goods and services in China for the China market, rather than for export. These are the manufacturers that have adjusted to China's higher labor costs and its growing domestic consumer market.

The benefits of manufacturing in China for the American market for labor-intensive low-cost items may no longer be valid; however, the efficiencies of the well-trained and lean China factory and reliable infrastructure may still be viable in comparison with shifting production elsewhere. For the large China market, it simply makes sense to maintain a certain level of production in China, as the logistics costs, supply chain, and knowledge of the domestic market provide inherent advantages. For the rest of the world, where unit orders are typically smaller in comparison to the United States, which is a unified market, the advantages of economies of scale of the China factory make it harder for a new country to compete.

HEY MR CONGRESSMAN

I've had the privilege to brief many American politicians during their China visits. What I often advise them is to focus on jobs. There are so many American jobs that are reliant on global trade. The United States is still the inventor and designer for the world. Often, the United States is still the source of power and money—and high-paying American jobs—regardless of where the product is made. If manufacturing can be automated, then it could be brought back to the United States. Meanwhile, most of the labor-intensive manufacturing will never be brought back, so why not take a more hands-off approach and let the market dictate where things are made? What some Americans do not understand is that higher salaries and benefits—our standard of living—have a cost and that cost is a key reason that non-automated manufactured goods like apparel, furniture, or bicycles can no longer be made cost-effectively in America. I am not referring to high-tech or dual-use products which could enable a foreign country to use to help their military. I am referring to the 90% of consumer goods that do not make sense to manufacture in America anymore.

THE IMPORTANCE OF U.S.-CHINA COMMERCIAL RELATIONSHIPS

The U.S.-China commercial relationship remains very important, for several reasons. Many politicians do not realize the size of the investments already made by American companies in China. Large-scale factories are not easily uprooted and moved to another country. Thus "decoupling," if that's where we are headed, could not happen quickly without devastating commercial consequences. Further, an often ignored and undercounted statistic is the number of jobs in the United States that are dependent on China-based facilities. Much of the research and design still takes place in the United States. Also, many of the more sophisticated and expensive component parts being assembled into finished products in China actually originate in America. To singularly focus on the value of the product exported from China to the United States is often an inaccurate accounting of trade values.

Politics aside, when American and Chinese companies cooperate toward a common goal (e.g., profit), there exists a bond of pragmatic cooperation. This cooperation allows for more people-to-people relationships to develop—and a common understanding. Essentially, the business people on either side become "commercial diplomats." I have dozens of those types of relationships and I am sure my Chinese counterparts do as well.

U.S.-China Risks

The Greek historian's metaphor of the Thucydides Trap essentially says that when a rising power threatens the ruling power it often leads to a dangerous confrontation. Much of the rhetoric both societies hear today is being trumpeted by those who stand to gain by such fear-mongering (military-industrial complex on both sides, news media, xenophobes, etc.).

From a global supply chain practitioner's perspective, we proactively mitigate risks and create a predictable and reliable business climate. As such, having an over-reliance on a single source—be it a single factory, single country, or even a single region—is not advisable. For years, many American companies had attempted what is called a "China plus one" strategy, i.e., having robust second sources outside of China, in an attempt to add agility to their business toolkit. The challenge had been that many of these efforts were wasted, as the cost of dual manufacturing in, for example, Mexico, was so cost-prohibitive (as compared to China) that it was not a realistic alternative for mass production for most of the industries already operating in China. Today, however, with the increased cost of production in China (driven primarily by labor, social welfare costs, and overhead, and then additionally by America's punitive import duty cost increases), that is no longer the case. Further, with improving infrastructure in, for example, Vietnam, certain low-cost production has indeed been successfully either dual-sourced or even entirely moved out of China.

Laissez-Faire = Allow to Do

Adam Smith's economic theory states that markets work best when governments leave them alone. As a global trader, I mostly agree with this premise (sometimes governments do need to intervene simply to enforce the rule of law and prevent fraud, corruption, and IP theft).

Artificial barriers to trade usually wind up costing the consumer. Today in the United States, one of the biggest concerns is inflation—especially as it erodes the buying power of the lower and middle classes so disproportionately. Therefore, I would like to remind the American policymakers that they should primarily strive to look after the welfare of the lower and middle classes and do what is right for them in the long run and to not necessarily make policy based on what seems popular today, especially to those with vested interests.

For the most part, I do believe that the Chinese policymakers, especially at the local and Provincial levels, do understand that there are benefits to allowing the American manufacturer to operate without overt interference in China. Most locales recognize their foreign investors as critical providers of quality investment, quality employment, quality skills development, quality ecosystem development, and quality corporate conduct. The concerns I am aware of mainly pertain to the protection of intellectual property, equal treatment vis-a-vis Chinese competitors, and fair market access to Chinese consumers. China's policymakers, who frequently survey the remaining American manufacturers in China, would be well-advised to pay attention to these points.

GLOBALISM VS PROTECTIONISM AND ISOLATIONISM

There is no question that we are now at a crossroads. George Washington, in his 1776 Farewell Address, said "the great rule of conduct for us in regard to foreign nations is, in extending our commercial relations, to have with them as little political connection as possible." This was not a call for isolationism; rather, a detachment of politics from commerce. In my opinion, politics should be and always has been about one thing: Jobs!

To be clear, I am a globalist and prefer minimal governmental interference in trade. Over 200 years ago, the classical economist David Ricardo's Comparative Advantage Theory suggested that a country should specialize in producing and exporting those products where it has a relative cost advantage and should import those goods in which it has a relative cost disadvantage. I believe this theory still holds true today.

Some people in both the United States and China are seeking to decouple the China-U.S. co-reliance. This is primarily a political, even xenophobic, preference. What many of these pro-decouple pundits do not realize is that the commercial forces had already started this process several years ago and that their government's intervention is not even necessary. As China becomes an even more expensive manufacturing country, multinational manufacturers will continue shifting production to South and Southeast Asia. The artificial push of punitive import duties is essentially just taxing the American consumer and this is unarguably one of the causes of today's high inflation.

In conclusion, China and the United States share the blame for congested ports, elevated freight rates, product shortages, and the higher price of consumer goods in the United States. These problems were primarily caused by soaring demand, lagging supply, and inefficient maritime infrastructure State-side. China is probably America's biggest ally with whom to address these problems. The premise of the China export machine of the past four decades has been all about low-cost manufacturing and efficient infrastructure. Allowing market forces to freely dictate where products should be manufactured tells us that it is time for the next countries in South and Southeast Asia to step up and claim their market share; however, without proper investment in modern factory equipment and efficient road, rail, and port infrastructure, their employment gains may be short-lived.

America's decoupling from China and on-shoring, near-shoring, or alternative off-shoring production may make good political sense; however, global trade is based on mitigating risks and reducing costs. Co-reliance between the United States and China will be naturally reduced based on a combination of efficiency gains in alternative manufacturing countries' efficiencies, as well as the use of robotics and automation (which diminishes the advantage of lower labor costs). As commercial relationships between American and Indian or Vietnamese suppliers grow, those bonds of trust will also develop. While China may not remain the factory of the world across the gamut of categories it has in the past, it will still play a vital role in the global supply chain for a large set of them. The reasons for this will be market-driven, not politically defined.

Daniel M. Krassenstein *is a global supply chain executive with 35 years of international manufacturing and logistics experience. As the Global Supply Chain Director for Procon Pacific, an industrial packaging company, Mr. Krassenstein is responsible for production and logistics of facilities in China, Vietnam, and India. His career has spanned decades in Asia and Latin America in industries ranging from ocean container carrier management, freight forwarding, contract manufacturing, and recently education. Today, he is based in Los Angeles but travels regularly to China and India.*

Mr. Krassenstein has served on the American Chamber of Commerce in Shanghai's board of governors, is active on the executive committee of the United States Department of State Overseas Security Advisory Council, writes articles for the Journal of Commerce, and is a frequent panelist on global supply chain industry events. He earned his Master's degree in Global Supply Chain Management from the University of Southern California, is a certified Lean Six Sigma Black Belt, and is a lecturer and adjunct professor at Cal State LA, UCLA Extension, and others.

CHAPTER 9

Epilogue

Kenneth Jarrett

At a time when popular discourse in the United States seems more focused on why American companies should not pursue business with China, *Selling to China* is a useful reminder of the depth of U.S.-China commercial engagement and the potential costs of taking economic decoupling too far. This book also stands out for another important reason. Each contributor has years of experience—decades, in fact—working on the frontlines of doing business in China. They are seasoned executives who have experienced good times and bad in China. Nonetheless, to a person, the authors—each of whom represents a different industry—still believe that an active economic relationship benefits both the United States and China. This should get our attention.

In fact, this book does even more. It holds our attention because each chapter provides fascinating insights on a key industry in China, giving readers a broad overview of the Chinese economy. In addition, each author relates their personal experience about working in China. Here too, we enjoy a composite picture, this one illustrating what it is like for

K. Jarrett (✉)
Senior Advisor, Albright Stonebridge Group. Washington DC, USA
e-mail: kjarrett@asg-china.com

© The Author(s), under exclusive license to Springer Nature
Singapore Pte Ltd. 2023
K. D. Gibbs (ed.), *Selling to China*,
https://doi.org/10.1007/978-981-99-1953-6_9

an American business executive to operate in China. Let me highlight a few of those insights before commenting on what lessons we should take from this book about the bigger issue of the role commerce plays in U.S.-China relations today.

First, for those who still think of China as a "copy-cat nation," i.e., a country incapable of breakthrough innovations on its own, that notion is debunked by several authors in this book. As highlighted in Bryce Whitwam's chapter on marketing and social media, China has been a bold innovator in the use of social media for branding and marketing strategies. Likewise, China's embrace of e-commerce has been faster and deeper than in most developed economies around the globe. Bill Russo's discussion of new energy vehicles (NEV) offers another example as he underscores the powerful influence of China's NEV industry on global trends. In this instance, part of the explanation is strong government involvement in a strategic industry, a particular feature of the Chinese economy, but it would be a mistake to dismiss China's progress on mobility innovation as the result of government industrial planning alone. The participation of local entrepreneurs and China's abundant engineering talent also explain the significant innovation that has occurred in China in this emerging industry.

Second, one can succeed in China without nurturing the competition and digging your own grave. Many foreign companies are fearful of this risk. What if they bring a good product to China, it gets copied and then is sold for less? Even worse, the local product might get better over time but still have the benefit of a lower price. For the foreign company, this could mean market share decline, including in your home market. In some cases, the foreign product disappears entirely as domestic players dominate the global marketplace. This is indeed a danger, but hardly inevitable. Plenty of foreign brands thrive in China even in the face of intense local competition. Moreover, Bill Russo's discussion of the auto industry reminds us that even when the intent of the Chinese government is for foreign companies to accelerate the development of local industry, things may not turn out that way. Foreign brands have dominated the China market for years and in 2022 still had a majority share—53%—of all auto sales in China. That market strength is even more overwhelming in the case of luxury cars. But that market dominance is now under threat as Chinese consumers turn toward affordable electric vehicles, a strength of local manufacturers.

A third theme of this book is the importance of government relations. Given the government's heavy hand in China's economy, the need to pay attention to government stakeholders should come as no surprise, but many foreign companies are slow to recognize this reality. This is especially so if the government role in your home market is limited. In China, however, the role of government is extensive. The government can be your customer, your partner, your supplier, your banker, your regulator, and even your competitor. State-owned enterprises compete head-to-head with foreign companies and even private-sector rivals can have a government dimension if the government is an investor. Whether the government plays just one role or many, it is ignored at your peril because the government can cause serious headaches for your business. Jean Liu makes this point forcefully in her chapter on education. Her industry is perhaps the best example of how a change in government policy can turn an industry on its head. The Chinese government's sudden announcement in July 2021 to eliminate the for-profit tutoring industry almost wiped out that industry overnight. Similarly, Mark Fischer's description of the NBA's travails in China underscores how even a well-connected and popular U.S. brand can be shut down if it falls afoul of the Chinese government, as the NBA did following a team manager's comments about China's policy toward Hong Kong.

Fourth is the role of culture. Chinese society operates according to its own rules and the same is true of China's business world. Foreigners must be aware of the key differences if they wish to succeed. Kenneth Yu, in his discussion of 3M's experience in China, offers a good discussion of Chinese politeness, the attention to protocol, and the importance of relationships, or *guānxì* (关系) as it is called in Chinese. Jean Liu makes the same point in her discussion of government relations work. Relationship building is a key part of conducting business throughout the world, as it provides the basis for trust that makes business possible. In China, it is often said that such relationships play an outsized role because legal protections are less developed. That may indeed be the case, but it would also be a mistake to believe that well developed relationships provide protection against all problems. Just ask the NBA. If you touch one of the third rails of Chinese politics—in the NBA's case, Hong Kong—you will quickly find yourself alone. In that situation, the passage of time might be your only solution.

Finally, a number of the essays discuss the current realities of U.S.-China relations and the negative consequences for the business community. This includes frictions over technology, as described by Don Williams; the rethink about supply chain philosophy, the theme of the essay by Dan Krassenstein; and looming questions about economic decoupling—how far will it go and which sectors will be most affected? Both countries seek some degree of decoupling, even if for different reasons. China does not want another Huawei experience and is determined to eliminate its dependence on critical imported technologies that put it at the mercy of foreign governments.

As for the United States, it does not want American companies to accelerate the growth of a strategic competitor. The Trump administration's redefinition of China as a strategic rival is a foreign policy legacy that remains with us today. In fact, to the surprise of many, and perhaps to the chagrin of Beijing, the Biden administration has been even more forceful about restricting the sale of key technologies to China.

Fortunately, there are few proponents of total economic decoupling. Most observers agree this is neither feasible nor necessary from a national security perspective. But even the current path of selective decoupling entails risks for the United States and those risks do not receive sufficient consideration. China is important to American companies not simply because it is an attractive market. For many American companies, succeeding in China is a prerequisite for global success. China serves as a supplier, a manufacturer, and an innovation collaborator. It can help companies in other markets and the revenue generated in China can enhance a company's global competitiveness. Even as the two governments try to limit collateral damage in the pursuit of selective decoupling, the U.S.-China trade war has resulted in unintended consequences harmful to American companies. As Bill Russo notes in his chapter on the auto industry, the trade war accelerated the decision of Chinese auto companies to go global to avoid U.S. tariffs imposed on products manufactured in China. This is not the first time we have seen this pattern. When the Obama administration slapped 35% punitive tariffs on automobile and light-truck tires from China back in 2009, the main outcome was to push Chinese tire manufacturers overseas.

Selling to China reminds us that succeeding in China has never been easy, but also tells us that many American companies have figured out how to prosper in this challenging market. Will this remain true in the future? Will China continue to welcome a foreign business presence? Will foreign companies still see value in maintaining operations in China? And how will public opinion, government attitudes and geopolitics affect the operating atmosphere for foreign companies? Just as the overall U.S.-China relationship is undergoing structural change, one must acknowledge that the view of U.S.-China commercial ties as largely beneficial to both sides is increasingly being called into question. This key foundation stone of the bilateral relationship suddenly looks very unstable.

There are reasons for this change. First, the nature of the bilateral economic relationship is different. When American investment dollars flowed into China during the years after China's WTO accession in 2001, the two economies were largely complementary. China manufactured at the low end and the United States was at the high end. There was little overlap and limited direct competition. From the very beginning, there were always points of tension for U.S. companies operating in China: investment restrictions, the risk of intellectual property theft, and unfair regulatory treatment, just to name a few. But the overall context for those tensions was different from today because the two countries largely operated at different ends of the economic spectrum.

Not surprisingly, China was not content to remain the world's supplier of clothes, toys, and low-value manufactured goods. Over time, China moved up the value chain into electronics, biotech, advanced manufacturing, renewable energy, new energy vehicles, high-speed rail, and aerospace. Moreover, it did so with the full backing of the Chinese government via a combination of industrial planning, state subsidies, and other supportive policies. One such initiative, "Made in China 2025," was announced in 2015 and identified ten emerging technologies with no obvious global leader. This launched an effort for China to dominate those technologies. "Made in China 2025" is just one example of how quickly China's ambitions have grown in the two decades since WTO accession. Consequently, U.S.-China commercial interaction has evolved from an era of relatively friction-free complementarity to one of widespread competition and commercial rivalry as China moved closer to areas where the United States has been the technology leader. Suddenly, the stakes became much higher.

A second reason is the sharp change in attitudes toward one another. There have always been ups and downs in U.S.-China relations: Tiananmen in 1989, the mistaken bombing of China's Belgrade embassy in 1999, and the EP-3 surveillance plane crash in Hainan in 2001. In the past, however, relations generally stabilized after a negative downturn.

The dynamic today is different. In both China and the United States, negative views toward the other side have hardened. In the United States, unfavorable views of China are at a historic high of 83%, according to an April 2023 survey from the Pew Research Center. Polling data in China is not readily available, but public attitudes are no doubt influenced by the steady diet of anti-American messaging propagated by state media—the United States as the instigator of the Russia-Ukraine conflict; U.S. military labs as the origin of COVID-19; the U.S. "black hand" at work in Hong Kong, Taiwan, Tibet, and Xinjiang; and the failings of an American society rife with injustice, inequality, and gun violence.

From my own experience as a long-time resident in Shanghai since 2005, I have felt the change in local attitudes toward the United States, although it is important to underscore that relations at the personal level remain friendly. Nonetheless, the respect and admiration that many educated Chinese had in the past for the United States has diminished. This reflects an appreciation and pride in what China has achieved and a growing skepticism that America has all the answers. It is also a reaction to the negative shift in sentiment among Americans toward China, which has taken many Chinese by surprise. The sharp drop in Chinese student visa applications in 2022 may reflect these changing attitudes.

Americans have far more sources of information about China, with the added benefit that it is not state controlled, but mainstream media in the United States suffers from its own lack of nuance. As far as many Americans are concerned, China is an oppressive surveillance state where its citizens are routinely shamed for jaywalking and suffer serious punishment for more grievous offenses as defined by the state. Even with an abundance of media reporting about China, it is difficult for Americans to go beyond the headlines and acquire a deeper understanding of what makes China tick, how most Chinese feel about their quality of life, or the extent of intrusion by the government or Communist Party in the daily lives of ordinary Chinese.

At the same time, it is important to emphasize that the negative views many Americans have toward China today are not simply the result of incomplete information or misunderstanding. Many of China's actions in Hong Kong and Xinjiang, its policies toward Taiwan, and its social tightening at home are objectionable. Collectively, these actions have created an unattractive image that overshadows China's many positive achievements. Americans are unlikely to think differently about China unless the country adjusts policies in areas where it is most resistant to change—Hong Kong, Xinjiang, and Taiwan. Thus, for now, it is hard to imagine any meaningful improvement in how Americans view China.

Similarly, Chinese citizens are increasingly convinced that the United States is looking to stymie China's development through restrictions on technology and other efforts to bolster the existing "international order." Among Chinese government officials, the sense that the United States has hostile intent is even more palpable and a factor in China's tilt toward Russia in the Ukraine conflict. On both sides of the Pacific Ocean sits a government that increasingly portrays bilateral tensions as a conflict over values and ideology. There is good reason for this, as conflicting values are indeed part of the problem. But the strong emphasis on ideological differences makes any kind of accommodation difficult, even if there are areas where a spirit of pragmatism might prevail. After all, why would one pursue any agreement with someone who represents a set of values inimical to one's own?

My intent here is not to get lost on a long detour about geopolitical tensions, but to describe the overall context for U.S.-China business interaction, both the increasing areas of commercial competition and the intensifying geostrategic rivalry. This environment is forcing each government to reassess what kind of economic interaction runs contrary to national security interests and what kind is benign. Or, to put the question another way, given that each side seems to have redefined the other as an enemy, how does the future look for U.S.-China commercial relations? Ten years from now, will there be a basis for a sequel to *Selling to China*?

I fully expect to see one. It is difficult to imagine a world in which the two largest economies turn away from one another. Even if we have entered an era of deglobalization characterized by efforts to enhance supply chain resilience and pay greater attention to regional economies, there is still ample scope for a vibrant U.S.-China economic relationship. This will require wise leadership and smart policies. As the sense of strategic rivalry builds, political leaders in the United States will inevitably take additional steps to restrict the sale of certain technologies. The United States is also showing a long overdue focus on strengthening domestic capabilities. The August 2022 passage of the CHIPS and Science Act, which provides $52 billion in incentives for the construction of new semiconductor manufacturing facilities in the United States, is the prime example. Chinese leaders will no doubt respond by emphasizing self-reliance and turning away from American goods and services. This is not to question national security as a legitimate government consideration. But where to draw the line? How can we meet national security goals without stifling trade and investment that does not undermine those considerations? And to offer a contrary perspective, is it not possible that increased economic integration would actually strengthen national security? Would not greater mutual dependency provide better incentives against conflict?

Most Americans do not fully appreciate the scope of U.S.-China economic activity and how it benefits American consumers. There is a general awareness that attractively priced manufactured goods come largely from China, but if asked to freely associate about U.S.-China trade, the phrases most likely to pop into the minds of Americans are "trade deficit," "loss of manufacturing jobs," and "not playing by the rules."

The benefits of economic engagement go well beyond stretching the purchasing power of American consumers. According to the U.S.-China Business Council, a business association, U.S. exports of goods and services to China in 2020 supported nearly 860,000 American jobs. For four U.S. states (Texas, California, Oregon and Illinois), China was the top export market in 2021. For 38 states, China ranked among the top three export markets. Moreover, the growth in U.S. exports of goods and services to China has been much faster than the global average. From 2011 to 2020, U.S. exports of goods to China grew nearly 20% compared to negative 6% for the rest of the world. For U.S. exports of services from 2010 to 2019, the comparable figures were 162% for China and 46% globally. China today is the third largest market for American companies, behind Canada and Mexico, and this does not take into account the annual sale of goods and services within China by U.S. companies from their local operations. Gavekal Dragonomics, a U.S. consultancy, estimates that figure as around $600 billion. That revenue also contributes to jobs back in the United States. Chinese multinationals operating in the United States also employed nearly 200,000 workers in 2018, according to the U.S. Bureau of Economic Analysis.

It would be a mistake for the United States to turn its back on a country that is already the top trading partner with 128 of the world's 190 countries and the engine behind one-third of global growth. Whether you are a soybean farmer, an engineer at Boeing, an employee at GM, Ford or Tesla, an employee at Apple or involved in the semiconductor industry,

China is critical to your business. Even, Starbucks expects China to be its biggest market by 2025 and home to 9,000 locations.

Finally, I would be remiss not to mention another important aspect of U.S.-China commerce, something that goes beyond the immediate business goals of profit and shareholder value—the people-to-people ties forged when conducting business. For most Chinese, their exposure to the United States is through brands, products, companies, popular culture, and tourism. In a commercial city like Shanghai, much of the white-collar working population is employed by a foreign company. Thus, even if U.S.-China relations are typically defined by political interactions at elite levels, for most Chinese, their direct exposure to the United States comes from commerce. At a time, when mutual mistrust is rampant and after a long period when COVID-19 travel restrictions brought most business travel and tourism to a screeching halt, the American business community in China suddenly finds itself with a special responsibility—to help Chinese understand what America and Americans represent.

The Chinese business community also has a part to play. At a time, when our two governments seem to be speaking different languages, both figuratively and literally, the two business communities are among the few constituencies still making an active effort to understand one another and work together. Whether in China or in the United States, our respective business communities must do more to articulate the importance of strong bilateral commercial ties and help Americans and Chinese understand how greater interaction, not less, is what we should pursue and how it will bring benefits to both our shores.

Kenneth Jarrett *is a Senior Advisor with the Albright Stonebridge Group, a strategic advisory firm based in Washington, DC. He previously served as President of the American Chamber of Commerce in Shanghai from September 2013 to December 2018. Prior to that, he was the Greater China Chairman for APCO Worldwide, a Washington-based public affairs consultancy from 2008 to 2013, and before that a U.S. diplomat from 1982 to 2008. During his 26-year diplomatic career, his postings included Consul General in Shanghai, Deputy Consul General in Hong Kong, and Director of Asian Affairs at the White House National Security Council. He also served in Beijing, Chengdu, and Singapore, and had several assignments in Washington, DC. He has degrees from Cornell University, Yale University, and the National War College. He is a frequent commentator on the business environment in China and has been quoted in outlets including Bloomberg, the Economist, the Financial Times, the Wall Street Journal, the New York Times,* *and Forbes, among others. He is the recipient of the Magnolia Award (Silver) from the Shanghai government and is a member of the National Committee for US-China Relations.*

Correction to: Selling to China

Ker D. Gibbs

Correction to:
K. D. Gibbs (ed.), *Selling to China,*
https://doi.org/10.1007/978-981-99-1953-6

The original version of the book was inadvertently published with the incorrect country name in copyright page, which has now been corrected. The book has been updated with the change.

The updated original version of this book can be found at
https://doi.org/10.1007/978-981-99-1953-6

C1

INDEX

© The Editor(s) (if applicable) and The Author(s), under exclusive   187
license to Springer Nature Singapore Pte Ltd. 2023
K. D. Gibbs (ed.), *Selling to China*,
https://doi.org/10.1007/978-981-99-1953-6

Printed in the USA
CPSIA information can be obtained
at www.ICGtesting.com
LVHW050301120923
757935LV00007B/257